NAIVE AND SENTIMENTAL POETRY

and

ON THE SUBLIME

MILESTONES OF THOUGHT

Friedrich von
SCHILLER

NAIVE AND SENTIMENTAL POETRY
and
ON THE SUBLIME

Two Essays

Translated,
with Introduction and Notes, by
JULIUS A. ELIAS
City College of New York

FREDERICK UNGAR PUBLISHING CO.
NEW YORK

Second Printing, 1975

Copyright © 1966 by
Frederick Ungar Publishing Co., Inc.

Printed in the United States of America

ISBN 0-8044-6821-4

Library of Congress Catalog Card No. 66-25107

To My Wife

PREFACE

The translations of the two essays appearing in this volume were made in the course of work on a study of Schiller's writings on aesthetics that has occupied me for some years of pleasant labor. The essays have appeared in English before only in the anonymous Bohn Library translation of 1879 which, apart from having been long out of print, is defective at least because of substantial and unindicated omissions in the text. This is especially true of *On the Sublime*.

I am glad to acknowledge the great benefit of discussion with my colleagues and students at City College, and above all with Professor Albert Hofstadter of Columbia University.

My gratitude is also due to The City College Fund for assistance in preparing the book for publication.

J. A. E.

North Egremont, Mass.
July, 1966

CONTENTS

INTRODUCTION

The presentation in English of what Thomas Mann has called "the greatest of all German essays" would seem to demand little by way of apology or justification. Yet while Schiller retains his popularity as a dramatist and poet, he is almost unknown as an aesthetician in the grand manner. Our tastes in aesthetics have moved away from "large" systems, like those of Kant and Hegel, that seek to display the close affinities of art and life, art and truth, of metaphysical and epistemological theories and the aesthetic perspectives generated out of them. Two more dominant approaches to aesthetics, both emphasizing a subjective viewpoint, have militated against a wider acquaintance with the poet-philosopher: aestheticism and positivism. This incongruous couple have shared the same major premise: that art and the beautiful have nothing to do with life, or truth, or politics, or ethics, or verifiable experience, and therefore the one argues that art and the beautiful have a unique significance, and the other that they have no significance at all. These findings were as familiar in Schiller's day as in our own and, in setting forth his program of aesthetic education as relevant to these matters, Schiller was forced to affirm:

> I hope to persuade you that this material [on aesthetic education] is less alien by far to the needs than to the taste of the age; indeed, to solve . . .

1

> political problem[s] in practice we must proceed by
> way of aesthetics, since it is by way of beauty that
> we attain to freedom.[1]

The vindication of the poet's, and thus of his own
vocation, preoccupied Schiller in the remarkable six
years (1789-95) during which he completely aban-
doned poetry and drama in favor of philosophy. The
reasons for this are so very complex and the principal
factors so intimately connected that it is only with dif-
ficulty that they can be extricated. First, and most in-
teresting from a biographical standpoint, comes Schil-
ler's extraordinary ambivalence toward Goethe. In
second place, generalizing from the resolution of his
conflict with Goethe, Schiller discovered that there are
two characteristically different types of poet and po-
etic modes of perception of the world: the naive and
the sentimental. Third, Schiller extrapolates from the
typology of poets to discover that the different kinds
of poets are only special cases of a more general
theory of human types. In this, Schiller is the origina-
tor of a theory of psychological types and has thought
through and anticipated a set of distinctions that have
proved fruitful in views as diverse as those of Nie-
tzsche, Dilthey, James and Jung. Fourth, as philoso-
pher, Schiller was concerned to resolve the problem of
the essential subjectivity of aesthetic judgment (as laid
down by Kant) so as to find some universally valid
foundation connecting the poet's private insights with
objective reality, knowledge, and morality. A full ex-
position of these four major areas is beyond the scope
of a short introduction, but something can be said on
each of them to indicate both the magnitude of Schil-
ler's undertaking, and the place taken in it by the two
essays included here.

Schiller and Goethe

Except for a visit by Goethe to Schiller's school in 1779, the first meeting of the two poets took place on September 7, 1788, but there was no rapport between them. Goethe saw in Schiller only the uncomfortable reminder of his own participation in the Storm and Stress movement, and their conversations were polite and inconclusive. Schiller felt he could not penetrate the bland Olympian calm that Goethe affected; his bafflement is amply documented in his letters to his friend Gottfried Körner. However, prior to meeting Goethe—at a time when Goethe was still in Italy— Schiller had met Major von Knebel, Goethe's friend and, in a letter to Körner, he gives a curious account of the Goetheans who had introduced him to the court of Weimar:

> Goethe's spirit has modeled all the people who belong to his circle. A proud philosophical contempt for all speculation and investigation is combined with an attachment to nature driven to an extreme of affectation and with a resignation to the five senses; in a word, a kind of childlike simplicity of reason characterizes him and his whole party here. They prefer to collect herbs or engage in mineralogy rather than to be lost in empty demonstrations. (August 12, 1787)

This passage suggests that Schiller's prejudice against Goethe was not due in the first place to any direct encounter, but to an antecedent feeling that here was a wholly different type of man, one possessing a character fundamentally opposed to his own.

Many years were to elapse before he was able to over-
come an antipathy of which Goethe seems scarcely to
have been aware (part of the difficulty, no doubt, lay
in Goethe's genial obliviousness in personal relation-
ships). The best description of Schiller's feelings is to
be found in another letter to Körner of February 2,
1789:

> To be often in Goethe's company would make me
> unhappy: even toward his closest friends he dis-
> plays not a moment of intimacy, there is nothing by
> which to grasp him; I believe, in fact, that he is an
> egotist to an extraordinary degree. He possesses the
> gift of fascinating people and placing them under
> obligation by small as well as great favors; but he is
> always able to keep free himself. He makes men
> aware of his existence beneficently enough, but
> only like a god, without giving of himself—this
> seems to me to be a deliberate and systematic mode
> of action calculated to indulge the highest degree
> of egotism. Men should not allow such a being to
> arise among them. For these reasons I hate him,
> although at the same time I love his spirit with all
> my heart and think highly of him. I think of him as
> a prude etc. . . . He has aroused a quite astonishing
> mixture of hatred and love in me, a feeling not un-
> like that which Brutus and Cassius must have had
> for Caesar; I could murder his spirit and then love
> him with all my heart.

The height of this antipathy is found in the indirect
allusions in *Anmut und Würde (Grace and Dignity)*
(to which the two poets never once referred in all their
subsequent years of correspondence [2]), and its final
resolution is in *Naive and Sentimental Poetry,* in which
Schiller finally found a basis for two such different
types of humanity.

The philosophical context of *Grace and Dignity*

shows how Schiller is led by his argument to the "harsh passages" bearing on Goethe. Schiller is working in his favorite manner: the exposition of two diametrically opposed positions, each of which is shown to be defective, followed by a dialectical synthesis combining the best of both and thus yielding a middle position. The first extreme position is *dignity:* the cultivation of a tragic view of life, in which man's only protection against hostile nature is his moral stature which vindicates him amidst physical defeat (Kant represents this position). The second extreme is *genius* which Schiller takes to be "a mere product of nature" (XI 208, 12). The synthesis is *grace:*

> If then, grace is a characteristic which we demand of voluntary motions, and if on the other hand, every trace of volition is to be banished from grace itself, we shall be obliged to seek it in whatever in voluntary motions is involuntary, but which corresponds to a moral cause in the mind. (XI 203, 21)

It might seem, from this rather tortuous passage, that Schiller wants to eat his cake and have it too. But what he is after is something like "the art that conceals art." Whatever is really spontaneous is "a mere product of nature" precisely because any merit that an individual's act might possess accrues not to the individual, but to Nature acting through him. It is only by exercising his own rational volition that the individual can claim credit for his actions (or be blamed, if they are bad). The genius (read: Goethe), however, is not such an individual. Although certain geniuses, Schiller tells us, try to dissemble in speech whatever they want to be taken for, what they really are can be judged by their spontaneous motions. The genius cannot display the requisite freedom which would

fulfill the moral aspect of grace because his actions
are an effect of nature which he cannot control.

Since genius is a gift outside of normal expectation
and endowment, a sort of free gift of nature which
Schiller felt he did not possess, he writes here almost
peevishly of the perverse thinking of most people who
prize genius more highly than the hard-won conquest
over animality and the common poverty of natural in-
heritance. He bitterly resented the facility and effort-
lessness that characterize Goethe's work, and seems to
have taken this occasion to allude obliquely to Goethe's
sexual escapades and to the even more irritating air
of natural aristocracy he affected:

> Both favorites of nature [i.e., the vegetable and the
> genius] are regarded, despite all their improprieties
> (on account of which they are not infrequently an
> object of merited contempt), as a kind of innate
> aristocracy, as a higher caste, because their advan-
> tages are dependent upon natural conditions, and
> therefore lie beyond any question of choice. (XI
> 208, 21)

The key to Schiller's initial treatment of Goethe lies
in his profound awareness of the difficulties of his own
achievements and his struggle to produce works ade-
quate to the ideas and ideals that prompted them.
Schiller's struggle is that of the artist who is all too
conscious of the extent to which his insights outrun
his capacities; he suffered from self-doubt induced by
the intransigence of his medium, too coarse-grained
and too charged with material connotations to bear
the burden of abstraction he would impose on it. To
friends in Leipzig he had written:

> If you want to show favor to a person who carried
> *great* things about in his heart and has done *little*

ones; who thus far can conclude only from his *stupidities* that nature has any purpose for him; who in his love *demands* terribly much and still does not know how much *he* can offer; but who is *able* to love something other than himself, and who has no more gnawing distress than that he is so little what he would like to be—if such a person can be dear and precious to you, then our friendship is eternal, for *I* am this person. (Letter to Körner, Huber, and the sisters Stock, February 10, 1785)

Slowly, and through a lengthy period of self-criticism, Schiller put behind him the more superficial aspects of this conflict. But the "gnawing distress" was no less acute for its increasing subtlety. Schiller was a genius to whom the notion of genius—with its tale of inspiration, of whole poems and plays *given* intact and wonderfully wrought, miraculous to artist and beholder alike, not laboriously planned and hewn out of recalcitrant and formless matter—was anathema. What personal merit can there be in the passive reception of the muses' whisperings compared with that effort? Genius may be a triumph of nature, but it is an affront to reason, to discipline, to sheer hard work. Nature is not to be relied on: the well, he darkly intimates, may dry up (XI 209, 33). It is in these terms that we must understand his relation to Goethe and to the type of genius Goethe represented, a relationship strained at first by mutual misunderstanding and what seemed a fundamental disparity of purpose and outlook.

Later, surprised by an illumination—"that is no experience, that is an idea!"—the way was clear for Schiller to subsume the two types under an even more general theory of human nature on an equal (or very nearly equal) footing:

> We shall be differently categorized, but in my most
> courageous moments I am convinced that our cate-
> gories will not be subordinated to one another, but
> instead will be jointly assimilated to a higher ideal
> concept of the species. (Schiller to Wilhelm von
> Humboldt, March 21, 1796, speaking of Goethe and
> himself.)

The famous conversation of July 20, 1794, which led
to the new understanding of Goethe and the theory of
types subsumable under a "higher ideal concept," has
been too frequently repeated for more than the barest
account of it to be needed here. Goethe's own words
will suffice:

> We arrived at his house, our conversation enticed
> me inside; there I was vigorously expounding the
> metamorphosis of plants and with a few strokes of
> the pen sketched the characteristics of a symbolic
> plant before his eyes. He heard and watched every-
> thing with great interest and a decided calm; but
> when I finished he shook his head and said: That
> is no experience, that is an idea. I was taken aback,
> somewhat vexed: for the issue which separated us
> was illustrated by this in the most striking way. The
> remarks in *Grace and Dignity* recurred to me, and
> my old rancor stirred, but I pulled myself together
> and replied: I should be very pleased to have ideas
> without knowing it and even see them with my own
> eyes. (Goethe's *Works* (Weimar edition) Series I,
> Vol. 36, 250)

The significance of this new insight, both for their
subsequent personal relations and for Schiller's philo-
sophical development, lies in a new discovery. In the
offending passages in *Grace and Dignity,* Schiller had
supposed a genius to be the wholly passive recipient
of ideas which he need not understand in order to
transmit them. Now he discovered that the alleged

"mere natural phenomenon," far from being incapable
of free reflection on what he has received, in fact
transmutes the content of his experience, *uncon-
sciously* supplying the human element of freedom in
the transformation of "mere perception" into a struc-
tured whole.

The origins of Schiller's antipathy to Goethe have
been spoken of as being rooted in a kind of envy of
the facility with which Goethe obtained his effects.
Not unmixed with this was something like jealousy of
his person, his vigor, his natural aristocracy, his suc-
cess in the world. All this compared very unfavorably
in Schiller's eyes with his own modest birth and de-
pendence, the difficulty with which he wrote, the care-
ful cultivation of unstudied ease in his work, his
chronic sickness, the constraint with which he entered
into personal relations. He was further stung by
Goethe's indifference—that of an older for a younger
man, whose name was coupled with his only in con-
nection with the Storm and Stress epoch they now
both despised. So long as Schiller conceived human
nature as corresponding to some single norm, he was
only too ready to attribute to himself whatever by
comparison he felt to be a defect. Yet the story of the
prototypal plant (*Urpflanze*) revealed to Schiller the
characteristic pattern of thought of the types that he
sketches in the *Aesthetic Letters* and expounds in de-
tail in *Naive and Sentimental Poetry*. So long as he
had thought of Goethe as wedded to the concrete
object and as receiving his ideas only through the
prompting of that object he felt a certain apprehension
for himself, and for Goethe he felt something akin to
the Platonic pity and contempt directed toward those
who inhabit the Cave. But once he could persuade

Goethe that even the most resolute naturalistic thinker must rise above the particular, and that the concept is the product of the mind and not of the world, the spell was broken.

Naive and Sentimental Poetry is the final product of an understanding that had long eluded Schiller. It is a matter of indifference to him, and one left in appropriate ambiguity (despite the later remark to Wilhelm von Humboldt, quoted above), whether the two types are ultimately referrable to some ideal notion of human nature in which the differences are reconciled. What is important is that the validity of each type is established independently of the other, and thus Schiller is emancipated from Goethe. Indeed, Goethe himself said that Schiller wrote this essay "to defend himself against me." But an important passage on Goethe in the essay provides little evidence of anything but admiration; Goethe is both the anachronism of a modern naive poet (XII 186, 21) and the naive poet who treats, in *Werther*, a sentimental theme:

> A personality [Werther] who embraces the ideal with burning feeling and abandons actuality in order to contend with an insubstantial infinitude . . . who in the end sees in his own existence only a limitation and, as is reasonable, tears this down in order to penetrate to the true reality—this dangerous extreme of the sentimental personality has become the theme of a poet in whom nature functions more faithfully and purely than in any other, and who, among modern poets, is perhaps least removed from the sensuous truth of things. (XII 213, 21)

Unfortunately for us, there is little in their correspondence to indicate Goethe's reactions. From a letter

of December 9, 1795, however, it is clear that until
he had seen the third part of the essay he was not at
all satisfied with the second part:

> I still have some misgivings about the conclusion
> [of the second part], and when one is warned by
> the spirit, one should at least not conceal it. Since
> the whole is so broad and sweeping, it seems to me
> on closer consideration that it concludes too nar-
> rowly and pointedly, and since this point comes
> precisely between me and an old friend, it really
> makes me a little apprehensive.

He then adds: "more about this verbally," thus de-
priving us of the details. Eckermann reports several
comments much later, but they lack the spontaneity of
first impressions. Asperity is, of course, not the only
sign of candor, but Goethe's allusions to Schiller after
his death (he outlived Schiller by twenty-seven years)
are a great deal rosier than those made by Goethe
during Schiller's lifetime. Perhaps Schiller's new under-
standing of him was not much more welcome than the
old misunderstanding!

It would, however, leave a false impression to sug-
gest that only Schiller gained from the friendship. He
was an "idea" man, and Goethe was only too glad to
acknowledge his debt for the wealth of suggestions he
received over a twenty-year period, during which
scarcely a day passed without a letter or conversation.
In a letter of June 13, 1797, Goethe sent some doggerel
verses to Schiller:

> In the wilderness the Lord was brought
> A stone by Satan dread,
> Who said: O Lord, Thy power be wrought
> To turn it into bread!

From many stones thy friend selects
A paradigm unmatched;
Ideas from you he now expects
A thousandfold despatched.

Dem Herren in der Wüste bracht'
Der Satan einen Stein,
Und sagte: Herr, durch deine Macht,
Lass' es ein Brötchen sein!

Von vielen Steinen sendet dir
Der Freund ein Musterstück,
Ideen gibst du bald dafür
Ihm tausendfach zurück.

Poetic Types

Schiller's defense of himself against Goethe consists in
the first place of the discovery that there are two major
sorts of poet—the naive and the sentimental.[3] The
naive poet is characterized by spontaneity, immediacy,
absence of self-consciousness, and a conviction of the
irrelevance of criticism to his work which, like a nat-
ural object, is simply there, without any purpose
beyond itself. In his moments of inspiration the naive
poet is in a "fine frenzy": he is an amanuensis to the
Muse, recording her mysterious and awesome whisper-
ings, gazing, when the fit has passed, in amazement on
what he has wrought with no less wonder than any
other beholder.

The sentimental poet's feelings are, on the contrary,
filtered by intellect, subject to critical scrutiny to test
their validity, intensity and propriety with reference
to some purpose extrinsic to his work. Thus the senti-
mental poet is mistrustful of inspiration; the critic in

him looks over his shoulder as he writes, controlling and correcting, assuring the conceptual coherence and consistency of what is said, gauging its moral and didactic impact, calculating his effects precisely in terms of some antecedently determined purpose.

Reciprocal criticism and self-justification by these two types are altogether at cross-purposes, since each judges himself and the other from his own perspective with little or no insight into his antitype. To the naive poet, the sentimental is cold and unfeeling, self-conscious and egocentric, calculating and overintellectual. To the sentimental poet the naive is irrational and anti-intellectual, irresponsible because indifferent to moral discrimination, subjectively immersed in fantastic intuitions which he declines to sift for their truth or falsity. The naive poet does not think about himself; but to his defenders he is the instrument whereby an ineffable and transcendent truth is brought to utterance, if not to comprehension; he is animated by an overwhelming conviction of the divinity of the intimations by which he is visited. Too close a scrutiny of the source would be rushing in where angels fear to tread. Carping criticism, with its this-worldly insistence on empirical verification and logical articulation, is the enemy of enthusiasm—of being filled with the god. To himself the sentimental poet is the imitator of a nature which he conceives of as the embodiment of a rational order of which the formal perfection of his work is the symbol. Feelings are always suspect to the extent that they are merely his, but if they have first been examined for the worthiness of their object and have been found to epitomize some universal human condition, then they attain the objectivity that is for him a precondition of their validity. Schiller's task is the vindica-

tion of both types of poet against the majority of crit-
ics, from Plato to the present day, who have defended
one type only to attack the other.

The first two major sections of *Naive and Sentimen-
tal Poetry* deal with the two fundamentally opposed
types of poets and poetry. The "conclusion of the
treatise" shows that what has been established about
the poets is only a particular case of the very gen-
eral theory of human nature which Schiller has
been seeking throughout his philosophical writings.
Thus, while the first two parts are of primary interest
as a contribution to Schiller's theory of literature, the
last part carries his philosophical development toward
its final stages.

In the first part, *On the Naive,* Schiller opposes
Kant's view by asserting the possibility of a naive art.
He treats the naive not as a defective, but as a legiti-
mate mode of perception, one proper to the genius as
the highest type of human being. The discussion falls
into three parts: a) the naive of temperament; b)
naivety and genius; c) naivety and society.[4]

a) *The naive of temperament*

All Schiller's longing for the spontaneity of nature is
brought out in the exquisite opening pages of the
essay. For the first time in his writings nature is favor-
ably contrasted with art, rather than unfavorably with
freedom or with form. This broad contrast is already
familiar from Rousseau's works, and is one of the
staple ideas of the Enlightenment. Art *(Kunst)* is given
the widest connotation, not limited to works of art, but
comprehends all those activities of the human mind—
social and political as well as artistic—which reflect
man's confrontation with his environment, his struggle

to remake the world as he finds it. Or should one say, as he perhaps once found it? (The state of nature, as Schiller points out in the *Aesthetic Letters,* may never in fact have existed—it is an idea only, like Goethe's *Urpflanze*—and for Schiller's purpose, as for Rousseau's, there is no need to establish that it did ever exist.)

Nature, then, is characterized in the first place by its simplicity and spontaneity. Provided that it stand in contrast to art, it is naive:

> Nature, considered in this wise, is for us nothing but the voluntary presence, the subsistence of things on their own, their existence in accordance with their own immutable laws. (XII 162, 3)

And art, for its part, is here man's whole culture or civilization. The appeal that naive nature has for us is not aesthetic but moral; for in themselves the objects of nature—birdsong, the humming of bees and so forth —produce their effect upon us not directly in observation, but mediately and symbolically, evoking a vision of lost innocence:

> It is not these objects, it is an idea represented by them which we love in them. We love in them the tacitly creative life, the serene spontaneity of their activity, existence in accordance with their own laws, the inner necessity, the eternal unity with themselves.
> *They are what we were;* they are what *we should once again become.* (XII 162, 23)

This is an outstanding advance on Schiller's earlier views of the relation between art and nature. It is no coincidence that in his earlier days, while under the influence of the Leibniz-Wolffian rationalist philosophy, Schiller embraced the view that art is properly only an imitation of nature. Even as late as the *Aesthetic Letters* an equilibrium of art and nature is postulated as the ideal of human nature, despite the acknowledgment that this ideal stands in perennial conflict with the actual conditions of human life in which nature and art are still thought of as necessarily opposed. In the present essay nature is a "construct," the product of an art which not only conceals its "artfulness" from obtrusion in the product, but also conceals its processes from itself in the workings of the naive genius's mind, so that the product appears as a product of nature. In the naive temperament these two concepts of nature coincide; but in the sentimental they stand side by side in violent and dismaying contrast. Nature appears in its purest form when, at the sight of children and childlike people, we are irresistibly drawn by the reminder of the state from which we have fallen. Our emotion is due to the awareness that in the child there is a potentiality to which no upper limit can yet be set. In ourselves, Schiller says, speaking with the typical oxymoron of the sentimental poet, experience has already corrupted the ideal; the child is a humiliating reminder of a perfection we shall not attain:

> The child is therefore a lively representation to us of the ideal, not indeed as it is fulfilled, but as it is enjoined. Hence we are in no sense moved by the notion of its poverty and limitation, but rather by the opposite: the notion of its pure and free strength, its integrity, its eternality. (XII 165, 8)

We are not confuse childishness (which is mere ineptitude) with childlikeness (which retains the purity of the ideal). Hence he disagrees with Kant on the nature of the naive, citing a lengthy passage from

§ 54 of the *Critique of Judgment*. Schiller breaks off the quotation immediately before a sentence beginning: "An art which is to be naive is thus a contradiction . . . ," perhaps to avoid too blunt a disagreement with Kant.

However, this is the point of departure for a new distinction which is more far-reaching than at first appears. Kant treats all cases of the naive as an unexpected rift in the mask of convention which prompts laughter because of unintended candor on the part of the victim whose real nature is thus revealed. Schiller adopts and expands this notion, which he calls the naive of surprise. But this is to be distinguished from what he calls the naive of temperament *(das Naive der Gesinnung)*:

> We ascribe a naive temperament to a person if he, in his judgment of things, overlooks their artificial and contrived aspects and heeds only their simple nature . . . The naive mode of thought can therefore never be a characteristic of depraved men, rather it can be attributed only to children and to those of a childlike temperament. These latter often act and think naively in the midst of the artificial circumstances of fashionable society; they forget in their own beautiful humanity that they have to do with a depraved world . . . (XII 170, 14; 171, 19)

The basic assumption here, although it does not yet emerge clearly, is that whatever is given as external nature does not determine the mode of its apprehension; this is a function of a natural endowment of temperament, and is a variable depending on the type of individual. It is not uniform in all rational minds, as Kant supposed. This is an anticipation of the distinctions to be drawn later in speaking of fundamentally different human types. For Schiller is arguing against Kant that there is no one mode of apprehending the world, but several. Some tentative formulations of these types have already been found in *Grace and Dignity* and in the discussion in the *Aesthetic Letters* of those dominated onesidedly by the form or material impulses.

In the naive of surprise the uniformity of conventional attitudes is imposed on a temperament inferior to them; but the naive of temperament makes its own, superior, conventions—their superiority is acknowledged (by those of sufficient culture and taste) just as soon as they are originated by the efforts of those with creative initiative:

> Hence it is necessary that nature should triumph over art not by her blind violence as *dynamic greatness*, but by her form as *moral greatness*, in brief, not as *compulsion*, but as *inner necessity*. It is not the inadequacy of art but its invalidity that must have assured the victory of nature; for that inadequacy is a shortcoming, and nothing that derives from a shortcoming can inspire respect. (XII 168, 16)

The unacknowledged point of departure for Schiller's remarks, despite the disagreements noted, is Kant's famous observation that genius gives the rule to art; and it is this context that effects the transition to the next major point: that all genius is naive. But without the distinction in the naive that Schiller has drawn, he would have been obliged to agree with Kant that a naive art is impossible. Indeed, that had been Schiller's belief concerning Goethe before he came to understand him. Art requires reflection and activity; nature (on the earlier view) is spontaneous

and unreflecting; the naive person, depending on
nature, is merely passive. Hence a naive art would be
riddled with contradictions: passive and active, unre-
flecting and reflecting. But given the new distinction,
passive and unreflecting spontaneity is safely relegated
to the naive of surprise; while the naive of tempera-
ment is active and reflecting (albeit unconsciously)
and is nonetheless spontaneous in its creativity because
independent of conventional modes of poetic invention.

b) *Naivety and Genius*

> Every true genius must be naive, or it is not genius.
> Only its naivety makes for its genius, and what it is
> intellectually and aesthetically it cannot disavow
> morally. Unacquainted with the rules, those crutches
> for weakness and taskmasters of awkwardness, led
> only by nature or by instinct, its guardian angel, it
> goes calmly and surely through all the snares of false
> taste in which, if it is not shrewd enough to avoid
> them from afar, the nongenius must inevitably be
> entrapped. (XII 173, 32)

That the genius is independent of rules was one of
the staple ideas of the period, brought out, among
many others, by Kant and Mendelssohn.[5] Schiller's
discussion, however, goes further than either of these,
because where they speak of genius only in connection
with art, he stresses equally the role of the genius as
one who gives the rule to morality and, as in the fol-
lowing passage, to science also:

> Only to genius is it given to be at home beyond the
> accustomed and to *extend* nature without *going be-*
> *yond* her. (XII 174, 4)

I remarked a little earlier that there are two mean-
ings of nature at this stage of Schiller's argument. In

genius, in the naive of temperament, they coincide; that is, the rightness of what is propounded either is, or seems to be, nature, to use Schiller's phrase. If, however, nature referred only to external nature as uniformly given in sensation, there would be no question of "extending" it. What is meant by "extending nature" is, I think, that genius extends nature as we *understand* it. The difference between the two concepts of nature is due to the different ways of apprehending it. To "go beyond" nature is to explain or describe in a way that falsifies whatever in the facts is uniformly given. This is the correlate in morality and science of the transcendent abuse of reason in the Kantian sense, and is due to the possibility that even the greatest genius may be perverted by the taste of his age, or otherwise be false to his own nature. But as genius he is not bound by the accustomed—he as unconsciously rejects the style and habitual outlook of a period which most people unconsciously adopt. The method of genius is, paradoxically, the opposite of method—he relies on flashes, and these are due in turn to "divine" inspiration, for "everything done by healthy nature is divine." (XII 174, 18)

The rules are no help: the conditions determining the greatness of a work of art, an ethical system, or a scientific theory cannot be defined in advance; they are a function of genius, which is as insusceptible of prediction as the acts of a saint. As the saint is a sort of moral genius, so the creative artist and the creative scientist are artistic and scientific geniuses. What they all share is an ability which defies analysis to strike boldly out on a path in such a way that we are enabled to see that, of all the possibilities, *this* was the right path to take. But this we see only after the event. To attribute genius to nature is to include it within the class of inexplicable data.

This is a far cry from the timidity of the pedant for whom "the sign remains forever heterogeneous and alien to the thing signified" (XII 176, 4), while the thoughts of the naive genius are "the utterances of a god in the mouth of a child" (175, 22) and they express (Schiller should have said, *seem* to express, but the metaphor is pardonable) the thing signified so immediately that the sign disappears within it.

c) *Naivety and Society*

Naivety is a quality of persons, not of things (177, 1): this precludes the attribution of naivety to the irrational or inanimate, thus disposing of the pathetic fallacy. The main danger of locating naivety in the object is that we may be led to the view that rationality is a curse, freedom of will a burden, and morality an impediment to happiness, for these are qualities we possess that are absent from the inanimate world. To those not confirmed in such an attitude, Schiller offers the Stoic advice to suffer what must be suffered as the ineluctable consequence of the imperfections of an actual society, but (and this would be a function of aesthetic education) not to abandon the goal toward which the actual strives:

> . . . with free resignation you must subject yourself to all the *ills* of civilization, respect them as the natural conditions of the only good; only its *evil* you must mourn, but not with vain tears alone. Rather take heed that beneath that mire you remain pure, beneath that serfdom, free; constant in that capricious flux, acting lawfully in that anarchy. (XII 178, 21)

It is most significant that the superlative qualities in nature, lost by man when he embarked on his independence, are happiness and perfection. The former will be mourned by the sensuous man, the latter by the rational. Happiness in itself is morally neutral, but not when it is the product of unthinking nature or of sensual satiety. Perfection *is* a moral category, and where nature is the symbol of perfection—as a harmonious unity of implicit order—it can stand for the highest ideal of quasi-divinity to which man can aspire. This is the attitude that Schiller attributes to the Greeks; in them, however, the attitude possesses the character of free choice unmingled with regret, self-consciousness, and melancholy—that combination which Schiller stigmatizes as the way the sentimental goes astray.

> . . . if *we,* in certain moral moods of the mind, might wish to surrender the advantage of our freedom of will, which exposes us to so much conflict within ourselves, to so much unrest and errant bypaths, to the choiceless but calm necessity of the irrational, the fantasy of the Greek, in direct opposition to this, is engaged in rooting human nature in the inanimate world and assigning influence to the will where blind necessity reigns. (180, 10)

The source of the quite different spirits which animate our age and that of the Greeks lies in our alienation from nature because of the conditions of our society. Only in childhood do we find a symbol of our lost innocence and directness; and we attribute our alienation to "grovelling reason." Needless to say, Schiller is not proposing as a corrective, a return to the state of nature, even on the Greek model [6] (this is a theme already touched on in the sixth of the *Aesthetic Let-*

ters). It is simply not feasible to pretend that no over-
all advance in civilization has occurred, even though
he does not deny that the Greeks were happier—"bet-
ter adjusted" we might say—

> Our feeling for nature is like the feeling of an
> invalid for health. (XII 182, 12)

Unlike ourselves, the healthy Greek did not have feel-
ings about his feelings. But the corruption of innocence
is evident even in the fourth century: Schiller contrasts
Euripides with Aeschylus, and he cannot find a naive
Latin poet to contrast with Horace, Vergil, and Pro-
pertius. What has been lost is the complete identifica-
tion with nature that characterizes the naive poet—the
unity between the poet and his work, between subject
and object. In contrast to this, the sentimental poet
senses within himself the divisive power of artificiality,
and seeks out the nature he has lost.

Homer and Shakespeare are the outstanding ex-
amples of the naive poet. Shakespeare is the subject of
a remarkable passage (184, 1), which simultaneously
reveals Schiller's classification of himself as a senti-
mental poet—hardly a surprise, but the only such
avowal in the published essays. The critical cross-pur-
poses to which he refers (i.e., the fallacy of judging
one of these mutually exclusive types by the criteria
of the other) led to a complete misunderstanding. For
at first Schiller had sought in Shakespeare just those
qualities which, taking himself as the norm, are the
last to be found in the naive poet:

> Misled by acquaintance with more recent poets into
> looking first for the poet in his work, to find *his*
> heart, to reflect in unison with *him* on his subject
> matter, in short, to observe the object in the subject,

it was intolerable to me that here there was no way to lay hold of the poet, and nowhere to confront him. I studied him and he possessed my complete admiration for many years before I learned to love him as an individual. (XII 184, 8)

Schiller goes on to contrast two episodes of knightly chivalry in warfare from Homer and Ariosto, showing that while the naive poet simply describes what happens, the sentimental cannot refrain from bursting in to comment in his own person on the moral beauty of the action. In an age as artificial as our own, the naive poet is all but impossible; and if one should occur (at last, the allusion to Goethe!), he appears as an alien presence, upsetting whatever arbitrary criteria the contemporary critics have assigned immortality to:

> The stamp of the conqueror is marked upon their brows; but we would rather be coddled and indulged by the Muses. By the critics, the true gamekeepers of taste, they [the naive poets] are detested as trespassers whom one would prefer to suppress . . . (185, 32) [7]

The Sentimental Poets

In the second part of the essay, Schiller reasserts what he has already set down in some of his earlier essays (notably in the *Aesthetic Letters*—see the 15th Letter, XII 55, 14): namely, the centrality of the poetic impulse as the means by which human nature receives its utmost possible expression. The two poetic types are now further defined with reference to "pure, not crude nature," a concept which is equated with the ideal of human nature as a balance of sense and reason ("crude

nature" is dominated by sense). A critically important
concept that has occasionally been used before in a
vague and colloquial way now receives a more sys-
tematic explication—this is the "mode of perception"
(Empfindungsweise). Since, as so often in Schiller, the
term is not very clearly defined, it is necessary to dis-
cover its meaning by the ways in which he uses it. It
seems to refer to the characteristic pattern of interpre-
tation which the poet imposes on the world. It is
partly a matter of response, i.e., typical feelings *(Ge-
fühle)* and reactions *(Affekte)* to the given, partly a
matter of *how* the poet perceives the world, not *what*
he perceives. The latter is determined by the categories
of the understanding and by what is given as matter
of fact—here Schiller has no quarrel with Kant. But
the manner in which the world is understood is a con-
cept independent of the categories—it determines at-
titudes, not facts.

The naive poet *is* nature (i.e., "pure" nature), be-
cause his characteristic mode of perception of the
world attributes to it the inner harmony and unity that
he himself possesses. Since that unity is indeed a unity,
there is only one mode of perception common to all
naive poets, however technically different the poetic
forms (ode, sonnet, etc.) they employ may be.

But the sentimental poet *seeks* nature (i.e., that
ideal unity) precisely because it is lacking in himself.
For him there is an immense disparity between the
ideas of infinite perfection he entertains about the
world and the finite imperfection he actually encoun-
ters. The disparity may be manifested in two main
ways which yield a multiplicity of poetic types. The
mode of perception may be determined either by the
repulsion he feels for the imperfect and actual, and

this leads to _satire_. ("Playful" satire, if the world seems absurd; "punitive" if it seems malicious.) Or the mode of perception may be determined by his attraction to √ the ideal, and this leads to _elegy_ (elegy proper if the ideal is represented as lost; idyll if he represents the ideal as though it were existent).

This results in four modes of perception for the sentimental poets. Schiller pays little attention to the subtypes of the satirical mode after he has defined them, and so continues to speak for the balance of the essay of three principal modes: satirical, elegiac, and idyllic. Before turning to a brief discussion of these, it is important to note a significant point in Schiller's method of treating his problem. Among his many talents, not the least is his capacity as an historiographer (it certainly outweighs the value of his actual historical writings). While many of his works, including the historical dramas, display a profound historical sense, he seems to have been very consciously on guard against the dangers of what has come to be known as "historicism." Among these dangers is the notion, to which unnumbered historians have succumbed, that some sort of binding pattern may be detected in the flow of events; and this is more often construed as a sentence than as a warning.[8] The present argument offers an illustration of Schiller's approach. Despite the fact that, on the whole, the naive poets are found in antiquity, and the sentimental ones in modern times, the concept of naive and sentimental in poetry cannot first be derived empirically by abstraction from ancient poetry and then be employed to demonstrate that naive poetry cannot exist today. This would be a "historicist" approach. The definition must be based on the characteristic distinction in human types so that senti-

mental poets can be found in antiquity and naive poets
in modern times, and even both types in the same work
(*The Sorrows of Young Werther* is, as we have seen,
Schiller's example of this). But the insistence that
poetry be addressed to nature must not be construed
as denying the right of modern poetry to the title of
poetry at all, even though naive and sentimental poetry
are characteristic of early and late stages of civiliza-
tion for the reasons Schiller gives in the essay. His
analysis, therefore, does not follow a temporal correla-
tion, but the modes of perception that characterize the
types. It would ill become the "poet of freedom" to
fall victim to historical determinism.

a) *Satirical Poetry*

The satirical poet may react in two ways:

> The poet is satirical if he takes as his subject aliena-
> tion from nature and the contradiction between
> actuality and the ideal. . . . But this he can execute
> either seriously and with passion, or jokingly and
> with good humor, according as he dwells in the
> realm of will or the realm of understanding. The
> former is a function of punitive or pathetic satire,
> the latter of playful satire. (XII 193, 21)

The poetic function may neither be dominated by the
"accent of correction" of the one, nor by the concern
for diversion of the other. If poetry is to be play, as
urged in the Fourteenth of the *Aesthetic Letters*, the
pathetic satirist, whose purpose in contrasting actu-
ality with ideality is to provoke amelioration of the
former, will be too solemn. And, conversely, the ridi-
cule which the playful satirist heaps on that same con-
trast, is too frivolous and may easily lapse into a mere
desire to provide amusement.

The pathetic satirist will tend toward didacticism, because to him the moral issues are of such paramount importance as to eclipse art altogether. His difficulty will be "to avoid doing injury to the poetic form which subsists in freedom of play" (194, 19). The remedy is supplied by a transcending of the immediate issues into the sublime. Failing this, the danger is that the opposition will not be between the actual and ideal, but between the actual (i.e., the external world and its demands upon the individual) and some frustrated desire of the individual himself. Presumably the decision whether a particular work reveals some special pleading on the part of the artist, or is instead an extraordinarily bitter but cogent view of humanity or of nature is in turn dependent upon the type to which the artist belongs.[9] Schiller's own criterion is clear enough—it is the ideal with which the actual must be contrasted, and the ideal is optimistically conceived:

> For if the emotion arises out of the ideal that confronts actuality, then all inhibiting feelings are lost in the sublimity of the former, and the greatness of the idea with which we are filled elevates us above all the limitations of experience. (195, 18) [10]

The intense and spasmodic nature of the pathetic satirist animated by the sublime is contrasted now with the harmonious uniformity of the playful satirist whose beautiful soul is reflected in the calm urbanity of his reactions. While the first depends on his subject matter to supply the sublimity that can inhere only in concrete manifestations of the ideal, the second supplies in his own person the beauty that preserves his theme from frivolity. This introduces, in a manner that has seemed abrupt to some commentators but is really quite relevant, a discussion of the relative merits of tragedy and comedy. For the same distinction applies here also. No doubt, Schiller says, tragedy treats of a more important subject matter; the theme carries the poet who is often overwhelmed by the sublimity of the material and is forced to appeal to his hearers' emotions. But in comedy it falls to the poet to save the subject matter from collapsing into triviality by appealing to the understanding. In a splendid passage Schiller confirms Socrates' hint (in the *Symposium*) that comedy is more significant than tragedy; and at the same time shows comedy to be one aspect of the reconciliation of naive and sentimental:

> Even if tragedy proceeds from a more significant point, one is obliged to concede, on the other hand, that comedy proceeds toward a more significant purpose and it would, were it to attain it, render all tragedy superfluous and impossible. Its purpose is uniform with the highest after which man has to struggle: to be free of passion, always clear, to look serenely about and within himself, to find everywhere more coincidence than fate, and rather to laugh at absurdity than to rage or weep at malice. (XII 198, 25).[11]

The section on satirical poetry concludes with examples drawn from Lucian, Cervantes, Fielding, Sterne, and Wieland, followed by a long statement on the essential frivolity of Voltaire.

b) *Elegiac Poetry*

The representation of nature as the ideal in opposition both to art (in the broad connotation, already familiar, of conventional civilization and artifice) and to actuality, yields the second main type of sentimental

poet, the *elegiac*. Works displaying this mood fall into
two groups, the elegy proper and the idyll. The mourn-
ful aspect of elegy is due to the dual sadness of na-
ture viewed as lost, and of the ideal as unattained. The
idyll, on the contrary, represents both nature and the
ideal as actual and, as such, an object of joy. It is curi-
ous to find two such disparate types classified to-
gether. But they are disparate only in the works in
which they are manifested, and not in the feeling that
underlies them. The interweaving of several themes
makes Schiller's point somewhat complex and it is
worth attempting an explanation, especially of the
footnote (p. 201 ff.)

The first of these themes is the historical: there is no
guarantee that a work originally conceived as an idyll
should not produce the effect of an elegy in an age
which has lost the happier outlook of the earlier
period. The converse is equally true: the elegiac poet,
provided he is spontaneously motivated by the con-
trast between nature and art, between the ideal and
the actual, which characterizes elegiac poetry, will
belong to this genus even if, as a result of a subsequent
change in the outlook of his readers, his work should
lead them to a feeling of delight in the seeming con-
firmation of their own temperamental predisposition.
The latter possibility may indeed seem less plausible
than the former to our own jaded age; but in each
case Schiller's principle, which applies to the genus,
will also hold of the species. The common factor re-
mains the preference of nature over art and of the
ideal over the actual. The causes of these changes are
not too well worked out in Schiller's historical theory,
but they may, broadly speaking, be readily assimilated
to the outlook of the *Aesthetic Letters:* the notion, very

similar to Hegel's, of a progress toward an ideal secured by the active participation of man's spirit in a scheme of which he is part, and which, despite temporal reverses, he is finally assured (if he only remain true to his nature) of attaining.

The second theme is the closeness of the idyll to naive poetry generally. It was made clear earlier that one cannot be a poet at all, not even a naive poet, if one is stupid and insensitive. The naive poet bears his knowledge so lightly that it does not figure consciously in his work—the processes of creation are neither perceived by himself, nor are they apparent in the finished product. The idyllic poet, however, cannot stop at this, but gives us his reflections on the feelings that the naive poet describes directly. But despite their differences, the similarity lies in this: that for the naive poet the gift of nature is his lack of self-consciousness; for the idyllic it is his sunny disposition.

The third theme is the objective-subjective status of the feelings in relation to the poetic work. This is especially problematic in the case of sentimental poetry of the elegiac genus, because the feelings in question are suspect for the very reason that they are prompted by the particular; yet they have to be justified in terms of the universal—an issue that does not exist for the naive poet. So long as the sentimental poet is bound in the first place to fix his feelings upon a particular object, his position is analogous to that of an empiricist who wonders in vain how one can proceed from an inductive generalization to the Idea from which the particular can be deduced. Thus Schiller sees the elegiac poet as susceptible of excessive abstraction which leads either to didacticism (cf. XII 206, 38) in the name of objectivity, or at the other extreme to a

totally subjective "musical quality" that lacks concrete-
ness (footnote, p. 209). The musical poet (Klopstock
is meant) produces a state of mind directly without
reference to a concrete image. One suspects that this
criticism, which is certainly overstated, is rooted in
Schiller's apparent insensitivity to music—he possessed
more verbal and visual than musical imagination, and
he feels the lack of some concrete prop from which the
emotion evoked can depend—presumably as an objec-
tive referent:

> As superb a creation as [Klopstock's] *Messiah* is in
> the *musical* poetic sense as defined above, yet much
> is left to be desired from the *plastic* poetic point of
> view in which one expects specific forms, and forms
> *specific for sensuous intuition.* (XII 210, 11)

Yet this is just the quality of music that so appeals
to those endowed with more musical sense than Schil-
ler; the whole argument between the proponents of
"program" and "absolute" music (as well as "represen-
tational" and "abstract" art) rests upon a tempera-
mental difference of type exactly analogous to the
objections raised here.[12] On this point Schiller seems
oblivious to his own requirement of avoiding critical
cross-purposes by judging one type by the standards of
another.

The last theme is a development of the didacticism
and moralism to which the elegiac poet is prone. Re-
peatedly, in all the major essays and several shorter
ones on this same point, Schiller expresses the view
that the poetic function does not and may not merely
subserve the moral. His point seems to be that poetry
will undoubtedly produce a moral *effect* if it is to be
valuable as art, but it must not proceed from a moral

intention. As presented here, the argument reminds us
that the true poet is pure and innocent and at one
with nature in its spontaneous decency (cf. XII 217,
12). He does not need the conventional morality which
is a social and arbitrary imposition from without, de-
signed to regulate the behavior of those who cannot
regulate themselves. Two criteria are supplied by
which to decide in the presence of some apparent
breach of decorum whether we should adjudge the
work by the standards of nature or of artifice: the first
is a sort of natural law argument, and when it fails
Schiller speaks of certain "liberties" being justified by
the poet's "beautiful nature," which, alas, leaves the
question equally begged. In the end, Schiller is forced
to acknowledge that while his criteria would rule out
flippant French novels and their German imitations, it
would also apply to some of Goethe's and Wieland's
works, and to this he "has no reply" (219, 28); in a
footnote he adds that this is a topic "on which I would
be glad to hear a reasonable opinion." [13]

c) *Idyll*

If the development of the whole essay may be
likened to a play, this section must be considered the
climax. For the idyll represents the highest mode of
sensibility available to the sentimental poet. The sec-
tion is, however, short because Schiller promises a
"more detailed exposition" which he never wrote. The
idyll is primarily concerned with the innocence and
happiness of man in a state of nature:

> The poetic representation of innocent and contented
> mankind is the universal concept of this type of po-
> etic composition. Since this innocence and this con-
> tentedness appear incompatible with the artificial

conditions of society at large and with a certain de-
gree of education and refinement, the poets have
removed the location of idyll from the tumult of
everyday life into the simple pastoral state and as-
signed its period before the *beginnings of civilization*
in the childlike age of man. (XII 222, 1)

But it is purely fortuitous and simply a matter of
mythopoeic convenience that the Golden Age is always
set back in prehistorical days. Such a correlation of
time and condition is more elegiac than idyllic, and
obscures Schiller's purpose which is to argue that the
idyllic state lies in the future rather than in the past.
This view has recurred repeatedly, with and without
direct allusion to Rousseau, wherever the notion of a
connection between civilization and lost innocence
has arisen. The ultimate reconciliation of sense and
reason is to be found in the specific rejection of the
argument that innocence can only be found divorced
from reason or from art or civilization. For Schiller's
optimism is such that only by setting this coincidence
of ideal and actual in the future can we reconcile our-
selves to the shortcomings of the present. In Schiller,
however, these two typical forms of pie in the sky cor-
rect each other, since nothing in the second argument
is permitted to justify the status quo.

Schiller now makes a distinction between the naive
idyll and the sentimental; the reference to a naive idyll
has sometimes been taken to be a mistake since the
idyll is a subdivision of sentimental and not of naive
poetry. But in speaking of a naive idyll Schiller is
clearly referring to the standard usage of the term as
it applies to the form of the *work* and not to the mode
of feeling. In this sense the naive idyll is timeless, since
the condition described is neither a lost innocence to

be mourned, nor a future state to be hoped for. That this is Schiller's meaning and not a mistake is made clear in the passages following this reference, in which he draws attention to the characteristically different *manner* in which the naive and sentimental poets handle their subject matter in treating this theme. The naive poet individualizes his material by presenting it together with all its limitations, but these are not felt as such; thus the infinitude of which the individual is a part is not fragmented (Schiller calls this "an absolute representation"); the sentimental poet idealizes his material by removing all its limitations—"the representation of an absolute." Thus the bucolic idyll is really only appropriate to the naive poet, since by the form alone he overcomes the inadequacy of the material. The sentimental poet cannot treat the same material with the same indifference to it—the very issue of its apparent unreason, bare necessity, and parochialism, becomes in him a source of melancholy for the reader who sees only an ideal irrecoverably lost. If, however, the sentimental poet does decide to attempt this form he must choose between the individuality appropriate to the naive mood, and the ideality appropriate to his own:

> If he is driven . . . to the ideal by the sentimental poetic impulse, then let him pursue this wholly, in complete purity, and not rest content until he has reached the highest. . . . Let him not lead us backwards into our childhood in order to secure to us with the most precious acquisitions of the understanding a peace which cannot last longer than the slumber of our spiritual faculties, but rather lead us forward into our maturity in order to permit us to perceive that higher harmony which rewards the combatant . . . [and] which, in a word, leads man

/who cannot now go back to Arcady forward to
/Elysium. (XII 227, 31)

With this most striking figure Schiller is done with
the assertion of what the highest aspiration of the
sentimental poet ought to be. The effect aimed at is the
same as that of the *Aesthetic Letters*:

> The concept of this idyll is the concept of a conflict
> fully reconciled not only in the individual, but in
> society, of a free uniting of inclination with the law,
> of a nature illuminated by the highest moral dignity,
> briefly, none other than the ideal of beauty applied
> to actual life. Its character thus subsists in the com-
> plete reconciliation of *all opposition between ac-
> tuality and the ideal* which has supplied material for
> satirical and elegiac poetry, and therewith all con-
> flict in the feelings likewise. (228, 23)

But the demonstration is lacking—the a priori deduc-
tion of the necessity of such a concept is promised but
not offered. Many commentators have remarked that
Schiller's fulfillment of the promise is not to be found
in another essay, but is offered in concrete form in
Wilhelm Tell. The time for philosophy was nearly
over, and the return to poetry as the only means of
rendering the universal concrete was at hand. The
defense of poetry lies on the borderline of philosophy
and psychology and, having ventured as far into this
obscure region as he needed, Schiller was ready to
abandon it for such expression of his sunlit hope as the
intransigence of language should permit. But he still
needed to explore the psychological distinctions im-
plicit in his views of irreducible human types, with the
possible expectation of discovering the basis of recon-
ciliation. To this problem he turns in the final part of
the essay.

Human Types

The end of Schiller's philosophizing is most unsatis-
factory for the philosopher, and has been almost uni-
versally neglected by the commentators. It is not so
much a culmination as a sudden stop on the verge of
an illumination which, once possessed, no longer de-
mands articulation—at all events in the language of
philosophy. This final vision of the vindication of
poetry requires and receives no explicit philosophical
exposition in Schiller, almost certainly, as I hope to
show, because the last inconclusive essays deny that it
is susceptible of discursive discussion. Philosophers
have always taken it for granted that the scrutiny of
first premises, especially of a metaphysical order, is
peculiarly their business; and most have further as-
sumed that it is also the philosopher who formulates
these premises, before they can be scrutinized. But
prior to scrutiny or formulation, in Schiller's view, is
their origination—and this, it turns out, is a function
of the poet, not of the philosopher.

The theory of types in *Naive and Sentimental Poetry*
illustrates two major aspects of Schiller's final position.
First, there are, as a matter of fact, at least two radi-
cally opposed ways of viewing the world; and what
has been shown of the poets is also true of men in gen-
eral: as witness the extension of the theory of poetic
types to the idealist and realist in the last part of the
essay. Second, neither of these opposed world-views
can claim objective validity, either in the "strong"
sense of the rationalists, nor in the "weaker" sense of
Kant. The evidence against the strict objectivity of the

rationalists is the impossibility of verifying our gen-
eralizations about the world against objective reality;
and against Kant the evidence is the absence of a
human consensus regarding the reality of the world as
it appears to men. Of two conflicting hypotheses, at
least one must be wrong; it seems to be Schiller's con-
clusion that both are wrong. In the essay *On the Sub-
lime* he advises us to take what he calls "the incompre-
hensibility of nature" as a principle of explanation.
That is, if we accept the notion that the external world
is strictly unknowable, then the status of our hypothe-
ses about the world is that of fictions, inventions, heu-
ristic devices to answer the questions we need to have
answers to in order to live; but the validity of these
hypotheses will depend on human criteria of factual-
ness, logic, and plausibility, and not upon their agree-
ment with an extrinsic nature.

What is the origin of the individual's *Weltan-
schauung*? For the majority of men, no doubt, it is a
compound of biologically and culturally determined
factors. Schiller makes no attempt to separate these,
but his discussion emphasizes the cultural factors. But
men whose world-views are determined by the en-
vironment into which they are born are victims of the
accident of birth and fortune. They are not free. If
this were all there is to be said, we should simply be
faced with the drab spectacle of another tawdry theory
of biological or cultural determinism. Yet world-views
change, and they are changed by men able to liberate
themselves from the thralldom of existing attitudes. It
is precisely because world-views are made, not given,
that the makers, the poets, all men when they exercise
this function, are free. To Schiller, the philosophy of
his day did not begin early enough in the process of

the production of these world-views. It seemed to him, viewing the differences in the philosophical schools that, as Bradley put it:

> Metaphysics is the finding of bad reasons for what we believe upon instinct, but to find these reasons is no less an instinct.[14]

Even Kant, with his glum view of human nature (to which Schiller had taken exception in *Grace and Dignity*), is guilty of the same error.

It is to the origin of world-views that Schiller addresses himself. Man's freedom, his most essential quality, is imposed on him because any account of the world in its totality must transcend his finite experience; and the totality to which his explanations must apply if their validity is to be objectively verified, is never given. Men are, therefore, free, within the limitations of what is given, to invent whatever schemes of explanation are compatible with those limitations. The philosopher, Schiller has told us, is a caricature compared with the poet, who is the true human being, because the philosopher seeks only to make explicit and to justify what he already believes, while the poet is not bound by his original endowment of temperament or the accident of environment. In his images and imaginings the poet explores the appearances of things unbound by antecedent schemes of interpretation.

These, then, are the themes we must develop if we are to understand the last part of *Naive and Sentimental Poetry, On the Sublime,* and the return to poetry.

This most brilliant exposition of the typological differences among poets is carried out almost exclusively in psychological terms, and culminates in the famous

account of the idealist and the realist. In the middle
part of the section two lengthy digressions treat once
again of the issue of vulgarity in art, repeating the dis-
tinction between "actual" and "true" nature; the second
deals with the hedonistic and moralistic views of
poetry, rejecting both and offering a synthesis. The
whole section is written in a single breath, as it were,
and is marvelously well argued in a style so pellucid
that any very detailed account of it would be super-
fluous. In some passages the language is so exalted and
the imagery so intense that one can go further than
those commentators who take this essay as Schiller's
farewell to philosophy, and see in it an even more
enthusiastic greeting to poetry.

The triadic structure of Schiller's dialectic is once
more brought out when he argues that naive percep-
tion corresponds to nature, reflective understanding to
art (in the broadest sense); and the sentimental mood
reflects the ideal in which the art that conceals art
returns to nature. This might imply that the highest
condition is that of the sentimental poet, which is
scarcely in keeping with the main theme of the essay.
But the ideal, as we shall see, is not so easily attained,
and not at all in the absence of the naive qualities.
That the two complement one another is brought out
repeatedly in parallel passages: the naive has the
advantage of fulfilling its objectives, but suffers from
their limitation and finitude; the sentimental under-
takes something infinitely greater, but cannot fulfill it.
The naive leads us into the fray; the sentimental dis-
affects us for actual life.

In the ensuing discussion of the purpose of art as
being either pleasure-giving or edifying, Schiller sug-
gests (XII 249, 21 ff.) without explicitly saying so, that

the naive mode of feeling is most closely associated
with the hedonistic; the sentimental with the didactic
point of view. In line, then, with his general tendency
to find a middle way, he denies the exclusive custo-
dianship of taste to the proponents of either view. The
workers are too exhausted, the intelligentsia inhabit
too rarefied an atmosphere for either to prescribe the
conditions of what is beautiful. Schiller evokes instead
the idea of the possibility (not the actual existence) of
a class in which the naive is combined with the senti-
mental—a kind of invisible republic of taste:

> For, in the final analysis, we must nonetheless con-
> cede that neither the naive nor the sentimental char-
> acter, each considered alone, quite exhausts that
> ideal of beautiful humanity which can only arise
> out of the intimate union of both. (249, 27)

Only such a vision is adequate to the poetic function
as it is consistently conceived by Schiller in these two
works. In their most elevated form both viewpoints
converge upon the same ineffable ideal. But this typol-
ogy is not restricted to poetry—the characteristic dif-
ferences between the naive and the sentimental poets
are symptomatic of a cleavage of types which is as
radical in every aspect of life. It is astounding that
Schiller should not only have seen beyond the demands
of the aesthetic problem, but that he should have gone
on in the conclusion of this essay to give such a bril-
liant exposition of a theory of types which exactly
illustrates his predominantly psychological interest in
philosophical problems, and to suggest that aesthetics
can never exclusively be a matter of philosophy. As
broad as the scope of the discussion of naive and sen-
timental poetry has been, it now becomes a particular

case only of the more universal distinction between the idealist and the realist.

The distinction is conceived in terms so radical that it seems implausible that any particular instance of it, as we must take the poetic types to be, could escape sharing the irreconcilable incompatibility attributed to it. The "inner mental disposition," on which the distinction is based, "is the cause of an aggravated cleavage among men worse than any fortuitous clash of interests could provoke" (XII 250, 15); it prevents the poet and artist from pleasing everybody and the philosopher from securing universal agreement; it means that the approval of one class will invariably bring the condemnation of the other.

> This antithesis is without doubt as old as the beginnings of civilization and is scarcely to be overcome before its end other than in a few rare individuals who, it is to be hoped, always existed and always will . . . (250, 28)

Outside of these happy few, Schiller sees little possibility of a general reconciliation, for he continues:

> . . . but among its effects is also this one, that it defeats every effort to overcome it because neither side can be induced to admit that there is any shortcoming on its part and any reality on the other. (250, 32)

By "abstracting from both the naive and sentimental character what each possesses of the poetic" (XII 251, 4), Schiller tells us that he has hit upon the more general nonpoetic typology of realist and idealist; most of the balance of the essay is a discussion of the epistemological and ethical (Schiller uses the Kantian expressions "theoretical" and "practical") attitudes char-

acteristic of the two types. Setting aside the specifically
poetic, and speaking of these types, Schiller finds that
the attitude of the (naive) realist in epistemology is
"a sober spirit of observation and a fixed loyalty to the
uniform testimony of the senses," and in morals "a
resigned submission to the necessity (but not the blind
necessity of nature: an accession thus to what is and
what must be." (XII 251, 6) In the (sentimental)
idealist these attitudes are respectively "a restless
spirit of speculation which presses on to the uncondi-
tioned in all its knowledge" and "a moral rigorism
which insists upon the unconditioned in acts of the
will" (258, 8 ff.). Each of these four points is then
discussed in turn.

The realist's epistemology is dictated by his view of
nature. The individuality of every particular event in
the world precludes the possibility that any formula-
tion of a law will exhaust the possible variety of future
events. Despite the causality and uniformity which the
realist theory of knowledge presupposes, those laws
must be based on experience, and strictly speaking,
they have no predictive capacity; indeed, any formula-
tion of a law applies at most only to the specified fac-
tors of a finite range of past events. This strictly condi-
tional attitude toward knowledge could be overcome
only by absorbing in the law the totality of all possible
experience. This is clearly impossible; Schiller suggests
that the realist in practice relies upon observed regu-
larities, but lacks or abstains from preconceived notions
in the presence of wholly new experiences:

> But since the sum of experience is never completely
> concluded, only a comparative totality is the highest
> which the realist attains in his knowledge. He
> founds his insights upon the recurrence which fits

into a law; but in whatever presents itself for the
first time, his wisdom returns to its beginnings. (XII
252, 33)

Schiller does his best to be generous in the matter of
the realist's moral outlook. As in his epistemology, the
realist is decided by reference to cases rather than
principles, which for him cannot be any stronger (and
may be weaker) than the cases from which they are
derived. From the idealist's viewpoint (i.e., Schiller's),
the will ought not to be externally determined; the
realist's will is not a pure will in the Kantian sense:

> From the individual case he draws the rule of his
> judgment, out of an inner perception the rule of his
> conduct; but by a happy instinct he is able to dis-
> tinguish from both everything that is momentary and
> incidental. (253, 21)

By his commitment to individual cases the realist will
get along on the whole without error, but he is cut off
from "greatness and dignity" which are the "prize only
of independence and freedom" which he substantially
lacks.

While the realist refers everything to the external
world, the idealist refers everything to his own reason.
He cannot be satisfied with conditional knowledge and
searches for the unconditional presuppositions upon
which that knowledge rests:

> And in this he proceeds with complete authority, for
> if the laws of the human spirit were not simultane-
> ously the laws of the universe, if reason, in the last
> analysis, did not itself belong to experience, then no
> experience would be possible either. (254, 15)

That Schiller himself speaks as an idealist is abun-
dantly clear from this passage, for nothing is commoner

to the whole rationalist tradition from which Schiller is still not wholly removed than this notion that the world is a fundamentally rational place; and human reason is of the same order as governs the world and thus can apprehend its reality. The definitive rejection of these propositions does not come until the latter part of *On the Sublime*.

Still, the idealist's first principles are less applicable to particular cases in proportion to their very generality. In explaining events in terms of the most general causes, he overlooks their proximate causes.

> Thus it happens that if speculative understanding scorns common sense for its *narrowness*, common understanding derides the speculative for its *emptiness*, for cognitions always lose in specific content what they gain in range. (254, 38)

In his morality the idealist is characterized by a rigorism which retains the impress of a conflict with nature. Because of his immersion in absolute principles, he is at too great a distance from the circumstances of the particular case. To perform a moral action he must exalt himself; he requires the stimulus of inspiration to bridge the interval between those principles and the immediate occasion for action. Thus it comes about that the idealist must be judged by these solitary acts of great moral stature, while the realist must be judged by the even tenor of his whole life. The latter will be functionally oriented—like Aristotle he will ask what a thing is good for—while the idealist, like Plato, will ask whether it is good. A number of other typical attitudes are listed; in general they attest to the realist's concern for pleasure and happiness, and the idealist's for the unconditionally good regardless of consequences. The burden of the argu-

ment is to show the onesided dominance in the realist
and idealist of an excessive adherence to the content
of sense and of the formal properties of reason, each
to the exclusion of the other.

The inadequacy of each view has been brought out
in rather more technical language in the *Aesthetic Let-
ters,* where the influence of Kant is also more direct.
In this essay, of course, Schiller's purpose is to urge
that for the integral completion of human nature both
aspects must be equally reflected. In fact, he contin-
ues, neither the idealist nor the realist maintain posi-
tions compatible with a strict account of their views.
The idealist abandons the absolute universality of his
principles whenever he undertakes some particular
action, however exalted; and the realist does not find
in experience the implicit presuppositions that make
that experience possible—the uniformity and continu-
ity of events in the world, the expectation that past
patterns of experience will recur in the future; a
wholly consistent empiricism, as Hume showed, is
impossible:

> In our account thus far we have indeed allowed a
> moral value to the realist and a measure of experi-
> ence to the idealist, but only insofar as both do not
> proceed consistently and nature operates in them
> more powerfully than their systems. (XII 261, 8)

How surprising Schiller's conclusion is depends on
how prepared one is for the exquisite irony which he
neglects to mention as one of the subtler characteristics
of his own type. On the whole he favors the realist as
more likely to fulfill the criteria of a specifically human
nature. Perhaps this is, as pointed out above, due to
an unavoidable mixture of idealism in the empiricist

position, while the flightier idealist lets nothing in actuality restrict his fantasy. But this praise of the realist cannot be bestowed indiscriminately; one last distinction must be made. There are caricatures of both types. The vulgar empiricist cannot proceed beyond the particular—his is an abject surrender to his own appetites and to the blind forces around him—he blows with every wind. As unfortunate as his condition is, however, the effects of false idealism are "appalling"; and Schiller's denunciation of the subjective idealist, whom he regards as a fanatic, is relentless.

It has already been indicated that the division of humanity here described is too radical to permit of a facile, or perhaps, any solution. That the types are commixed in practice is as readily conceded as that their complete fusion is impossible except as an ideal for all, and as a rare sport of nature in a few individuals. Indeed, the purpose of this essay, unlike the ambitious attempt in his earlier "Kallias Letters" to found an objective theory of beauty, is more touching and more modest: in the first place it is no more than Schiller's effort to understand himself and to overcome the sense that in being different from Goethe he was not necessarily worse. The scrupulous and searching criticism of his own type brought him finally to terms with his own nature: he is an idealist beyond question, but with a sober leavening of realism.

But this biographical interest is by no means the most important and valuable part of Schiller's objectives in these essays. It is still necessary to clarify the metaphysical basis of Schiller's position. This is to be found in a rather unexpected and relatively neglected source, the theory of the sublime; this brings out and develops the hints found in the comparative treatment of the metaphysics of the idealist and realist. I hope to show that in the implications of the theory of the sublime it is possible to find the principles which unify Schiller's theories of nature and human nature, of aesthetic education (including the key notions of semblance and play) and the archetypes of human temperament, and of his own disparate combination of idealism and realism.

On the Sublime

Compare these two passages:

> . . . if the laws of the human spirit were not simultaneously the laws of the universe . . . then no experience would be possible either. (*Naive and Sentimental Poetry*, XII 254, 16)

> It is precisely the entire absence of a purposive bond among this press of appearances by which they are rendered unencompassable and useless for the understanding (which is obliged to adhere to this kind of bond) that makes them an all the more striking image for pure reason, which finds in just this wild incoherence of nature the depiction of her own independence of natural conditions. (*On the Sublime*, XII 276, 13)

The first of these views reflects the still basically rationalistic tendency of Schiller's mind which assumes an accordance between man's understanding of the world and the world as it really is; the second as firmly rejects the notion that there is any necessary connection between those explanations and extrinsic nature. This metaphysical shift, the last in a long series stretching throughout his career, explains, I believe, Schiller's return to poetry if it is taken in conjunction with the vindication of the poet as the highest kind of human being, as argued in *Naive and Sentimental Poetry*.

The treatment of the sublime, usually in contrast with the beautiful, is a commonplace of the eighteenth century. Among the most famous of the essays dedicated to this well-worn theme are those by Hume, Burke, and Kant. Schiller's first effort along these lines (somewhat confusingly entitled *Of the Sublime*) so closely followed Kant's discussion in the *Critique of Judgment* that this may have been the reason for its omission from the collected writings he published in his lifetime. The root distinction common to these essays is that the beautiful is merely pleasing, the sublime awes and overwhelms by the sense of size, power, and majesty infused in the beholder at the sight of the vast order of nature, or of some of her works. This may have an old-fashioned ring, but it does not really; what has changed is the vocabulary, not the concept. Modern writers who speak of "nausea," "anguish," "forlornness," and so on, are referring to the same matters; only they have chosen the pessimistic reverse, rather than the optimistic obverse, of the same coin. The puniness of man, compared with the immensity of the universe he contemplates, is common to both eras. The differences are, however, significant, and not least for the bearing they have in Schiller's second work on the sublime, the one we are concerned with here. The eighteenth century could afford to be optimistic in face of the sublime because it possessed the metaphysical assurance of the first passage quoted above. Kant's famous remark that "two things fill my mind with awe: the starry firmament above and the moral law within," epitomizes the confidence of his age. So long as men

believed that the cosmos was rationally governed in
a way that must ultimately yield to rational under-
standing, the comparison between man's slight physi-
cal powers and the magnitude of nature's was not
unflattering. But in our century that confidence has
been lost; contemplation of the universe yields assur-
ance only of absurdity, and inward contemplation re-
veals the iceberg unconscious, nine-tenths irrational
appetite. The catalyst for this metaphysical change
was, paradoxically enough, Kant himself, and the first
thinker of consequence to be affected by it was Schil-
ler; he accepted the strict unknowability of the thing-
in-itself, but rejected the pessimistic consequences.

The first part of *On the Sublime* begins substantially
with the repetition of the views of the major essays.
No man, we are told, is forced to yield to force. Alone
among the creatures of nature man claims freedom
from external restraint even though he is subject to
forces greater than his own. There are two ways in
which education or culture set man at liberty to assert
his will: "realistically" and "idealistically." Realisti-
cally, by "physical education," man opposes force by
force (i.e., by technological advances); but this can
only be done up to a certain point (XII 265, 28),
beyond which man remains subject to nature. It would
be trifling to suppose that by "physical education"
(physische Kultur), Schiller is referring to gymnastics;
he means that development of science that leads to an
increasing control of the physical environment. But
beyond the limits of such achievements it is only ideal-
istically, by "withdrawing" from nature, by means of
moral education can man remain exempt from the vio-
lence of nature and secure his freedom in the fullest
sense:

> The morally cultivated man, and only he, is wholly
> free. Either he is superior to nature in force, or he
> is at one with her. Nothing that she can do to him
> is violence, for before it reaches him it has become
> *his own action,* and dynamic nature never reaches
> him because he has by his own free act separated
> himself from everything that she can reach. (266, 8)

The combination of these characters is found in the
sublime (or heroic) disposition which is that frame of
mind concerned not whether the good and beautiful
exist in the abstract sense, but rather that the existent
should be beautiful and good.

This sublime mood retains the characteristics of the
realist with none of his limitations. The idealist, on the
contrary, is certain to find nothing wholly satisfactory
in the world, and will fall prey to all the dangers of
hyper-aestheticism and what Schiller calls "melting
beauty," or his withdrawal will be the world-denying
stoicism (familiar enough in Christianity) which seeks
consolation in the afterlife. But the sublime, while it
seeks to be wholly free of nature—it is the pure spirit
acting by its own laws—is not to be construed in terms
of the "monkish virtues." It gives rise to a mixed feel-
ing of pain and joy due to the joint presence of the
two natures which are to be combined: the autonomy
of the morally unconditioned and the limitations im-
posed by external necessity.

> In the beautiful, reason and sensuousness are in uni-
> son, and only for the sake of this harmony does it
> possess any charm for us. Through beauty alone,
> then, we should never discover that we are destined
> and able to demonstrate ourselves as pure intelli-
> gences. But in the sublime, however, reason and
> sensuousness do *not* accord, and precisely in this
> contradiction between the two lies the magic with
> which it captures our minds. (XII 270, 19)

The material of the essay so far has been very much along Kantian lines, especially reflecting Kant's sublime of quantity. That is, the disparity of sense and reason described display phenomena in the world palpable to sense but transcending our rational powers to comprehend. Now Schiller introduces some fresh material of so radically different a tone that I am convinced that it must have been a later addition to the essay, probably a new ending prepared just before publication in 1801.[15] The point of departure is indeed, as in Kant, the wildness and majesty of nature; but it surpasses the ideas on the realist position of *Naive and Sentimental Poetry* in an extraordinary development of which only a few hints appear in that essay and in the *Aesthetic Letters*.[16]

This new approach is presented in the sublime of the incomprehensible. Unlike the sublime of quantity which cannot be grasped by the imagination, the sublime of the incomprehensible represents the vastness of nature which cannot be grasped by the understanding, and thus stands as a symbol of the supersensuous: for, like the supersensuous, the totality of the empirical world can only be approached, not attained. No doubt, to the extent that the world is understood and largely controllable, it is more convenient and agreeable, "but man has a need beyond living and securing his welfare, and a quite other destiny than to comprehend the phenomena which surround him" (XII 275, 26). This is a quite extraordinary observation in itself, but it is coupled with an attack on the rationalist position. For the rationalist who is determined to impose order on the world must presumably find that order either in himself or in the world. Generally he will claim that there is no possible disparity between the two, because, as we pointed out earlier, he holds reason in man and reason in the world to be of the same kind. To argue otherwise seems to the rationalist to destroy the certainty or even the possibility of objective knowledge altogether and, still worse, to deny a rational order to the world. What happens to the rationalist, Schiller says, when he fails to find the desired order in the physical world, is that he either defers rational perfection to the afterlife, or translates it to a higher sphere. These alternatives represent the religious and the Platonic solutions to the problem of evil. It is clear that in this vein of realism Schiller is convinced that anyone who really looks at the world will find enough disorder and chance occurrence to prevent the placid assumptions of the rationalist. He does, however, underrate some of the subtler aspects of the religious argument; though he does see, as the rationalist does not, the feasibility of maintaining both positions at once, i.e., both the actual disorder ("this lawless chaos of appearances" XII 276, 10; "the evil fatality" 280, 5), and the ideal order to which men are driven. But in his own day Schiller was much more likely to encounter complacency than *Problematik* in religion: the argument from design, despite Hume's devastating critique, was often heard, as well as the flat denial of the possibility of evil, or the claim of the necessity of limited evil, arising out of the loss of perfection from Creator to creation. Schiller's point of departure, in contrast to these facile solutions, is that the problem of evil, as of the validation of objective schemes of knowledge, is in principle inexplicable. Nature is as inscrutable to man as Moby Dick was to Ahab; and like Ahab we may, if we are not on guard, fall victim to the meaning we read into nature.

In the discussion that follows, Schiller almost exactly
reproduces what in modern philosophy is called con-
ventionalism or fictionalism. There is, of course, always
the danger in interpreting an earlier thinker of finding
in him anticipations of later developments of which he
had no notion and which, if he could speak, he would
indignantly deny. The plausibility of my interpretation
must rest on the evidence of the essay under review
and on the coherence of the explanation of the major
problem. This is to account for the abandonment of
philosophy following this essay as abruptly as he had
abandoned poetry to take up philosophy in 1789.

Schiller does not deny an order to nature *as a whole,*
but allows that chance [17] plays a great and unavoid-
able role in particular events. What he does deny is
any necessary connection between that rational order
and man's cognitive schemes, or as he puts it, "natural
necessity has entered into no compact with man" (XII
278, 34). Here he is more interested in the moral than
the epistemological implications, however. If every-
thing were cut and dried and "run like a solid busi-
ness," then we should have little claim to assert our
own moral freedom and independence within a totally
determinate system. For if our experience of external
nature were to constitute the whole basis of our ex-
perience, then we should be obliged to conclude that
we are as determined as the rest of the system (as
indeed materialists do conclude). Moreover, wherever
we supposed we were acting from freedom of choice
this would be an illusion based merely on our igno-
rance of determinate factors; and one must expect that
the area of free choice will shrink as factual knowl-
edge advances. This is the case to the extent that mat-
ters of fact are involved. We may freely decide to do

all sorts of things only to be brought up short by the facts! The kind of ignorance Schiller is concerned with is, however, not the unknown, but the unknowable— it is the essential impossibility of verifying the *interpretation* of those facts against an unknowable external nature which imposes on us the requirement, if we are to be human (i.e., to have more than an ephemeral interest in the world of appearances) to supply interpretations which are our free constructs precisely because they are *not* given in experience:

> If, however, [man] willingly abandons the attempt to assimilate this lawless chaos of appearances to a cognitive unity, he will abundantly regain in another direction what he has lost in this. It is precisely the entire absence of a purposive bond among this press of appearances by which they are rendered unencompassable and useless for the understanding (which is obliged to adhere to this kind of bond) that makes them an all the more striking image for pure reason which finds in just this wild incoherence of nature the depiction of her own independence of natural conditions. (XII 276, 10)

There is, Schiller claims, an analogy between the absence of a wholly discoverable order in the world (and therewith the real or seeming independence of individual events) [18] and man's moral freedom such that the former can stand as a symbol of the latter:

> For if the connection between a series of objects is abstracted, one is left with the concept of independence which coincides surprisingly with the pure rational concept of freedom. (276, 21)

We must point out the ideal content of this view and its relation to conventionalist empiricism. In general the empiricist is intolerant of the idealist assertion of a perfect rational order as being at best irrelevant and, at worst, inimical to inquiry into events in the world of experience (the only world he believes he inhabits). Against this, Schiller has already argued in *Naive and Sentimental Poetry* (XII 260, 8) that the realist is bound to include in his system ideas concerning the regularity of the world as a whole which go beyond the finite experience to which his system is supposed to be limited. That this is a further development of the insight into Goethe's mode of perception is clear enough: Goethe's archetypal plant, which he took to be an empirical generalization, was indeed an idea! In this essay Schiller recurs to this argument:

> Indeed, nothing at all can be truly called idealistic if it is not in actuality unconsciously employed by the complete realist, and denied by him only by a misunderstanding. (266, 35)

For Schiller takes the ideal seriously, not, indeed, as an actuality, nor as a substitute for actuality, nor even as a possibility to be attained, but as the bootstrap, as it were, by which we elevate ourselves and mark any advance in civilization. That such an ideal shares with the structure of cognition the characteristic of being our own invention both weakens and strengthens it in just the way indicated in the passage quoted a little above (270, 19). It weakens the ideal because it bears no necessary relation to the cosmos to which it purports to apply; it strengthens us, confirming us in the cognitive, moral, and aesthetic independence and freedom which, more than anything else, is the focus of Schiller's whole position.

> Thus reason combines in a single unity of thought within this idea of freedom, which she supplies from

her own resources, what understanding can never combine in a unity of experience; by this idea she subordinates the infinite play of appearances to herself, and simultaneously asserts her power over the understanding as a sensuously limited faculty. If one now recalls how valuable it must be for a rational being to be aware of his independence of natural laws, one can grasp how it happens that individuals of a sublime temperamental disposition think themselves recompensed for every cognitive misjudgment by this idea of freedom which is offered them. (XII 276, 24)

Then, Schiller continues, let us rather take the incomprehensibility of the world as a principle of explanation. The very fact that experience shows the indifference of nature to the rules we purport to derive from her in itself leads us no longer to expect to find the infinite in the actual and conditional, and impels us toward the ideal and absolute which we ourselves originate. The wanton destructiveness and unpredictability of nature make a special demand on man to insulate himself from her effects, and his moral dignity and sublimity subsist precisely in the stoic grandeur with which he "takes refuge in the sacred freedom of the spirit." (279, 5)

Then away with falsely construed forebearance and vapidly effeminate taste which cast a veil over the solemn face of necessity and, in order to curry favor with the senses, *counterfeit* a harmony between good fortune and good behavior of which not a trace is to be found in the actual world. Let us stand face to face with the evil fatality. Not in ignorance of the dangers which lurk about us—for finally there must be an end to ignorance—only in *acquaintance* with them lies our salvation. (279, 37)

Schiller turns briefly to the connection between the

sublime and the pathetic as they coincide in tragedy.
What the pathetic in tragedy shows is an artificial mis-
fortune which is the semblance of the real misfortune
commonly experienced in actual life. It has already
been argued (270, 34) that in the case of good fortune
the moral issue is clouded because (as with Job)
when things go well one cannot tell whether reward is
due to merit or merit is shown by reward—surely the
most detestable kind of complacency is that which
assumes that one must be virtuous or one could not be
rich. The moral issue is, however, directly joined when
misfortune is, so far as we can tell, unmerited. The
value of tragedy as part of aesthetic education lies in
its representation of misfortune in such a way that we
become practised in the elevation of the craven re-
sponse of defeat in the sensuous world into moral dig-
nity in the ideal world:

> . . . should an imaginary and artificial misfortune
> turn into a real one, the mind is able to treat it as
> an artificial one and—the most exalted inspiration of
> human nature!—to transform actual suffering into
> sublime emotion. Thus one can call the pathetic an
> inoculation against ineluctable destiny by which it is
> deprived of its malevolence, and its attack diverted
> to the stronger side of man. (XII 279, 28)

No tragedy is too deep, no injustice so triumphant,
that from it the lesson cannot be learned of the impla-
cable indifference of nature to our aspirations. And to
our intimations of beauty the fearful sublimity of that
lesson must be joined to complete man's aesthetic edu-
cation; for only by rising out of the limitations of the
actual can one find freedom in the ideal. Art is better
equipped to perform this because of the free contem-
plation of semblance independent of the "contingent

limitations" (282, 10) of the actual which distinguishes the aesthetic from all other modes of viewing the world.

It may not be immediately apparent how the conclusions of this extraordinary last essay of Schiller's are connected with the poetic and human typologies, and with his theory of aesthetic education; to this I now turn.

Philosophical Implications

If Schiller was diverted from poetry to philosophy in order to justify the poet's and therewith his own vocation, he returned to poetry because he discovered that philosophy was incapable of fulfilling a task much better suited to poetry. It is left to poetry, or rather to the aesthetic element in all forms of human expression, to carry out that task: the channeling of the natural gifts by which alone the ideal can be embodied and exemplified.

The blend of conventionalism and idealism that has been noted in these essays appears in Schiller's treatment of cognitive, moral, and aesthetic principles. The inconclusiveness of these principles in any demonstrative sense leads to the account of psychological types as the source of the inconclusiveness. Since the natural endowment of temperament is taken to be prior to and determinative of philosophical argument, the corrective to this determination must be sought in aesthetic education and not in philosophy proper. A later age broadened philosophy to include the subject matter of Schiller's enquiry: Dilthey calls this "philosophy of philosophy," and, acknowledging his debt to Schil-

ler,[19] derives types of philosophy from types of society;
the pragmatists, especially Peirce and James, also
engaged in metaphilosophical enquiry, and decided
the merits of philosophical systems with reference to
their consequences. But Schiller was never able to
overcome his belief (based on the dominant rational-
ism of his day) that the business of philosophy is to
convince universally (cf. *Naive and Sentimental Po-
etry*, XII 250, 18); seeing that this could not be done,
he was led to launch an implied (and in places, as in the
famous quarrel with Fichte, explicit) attack on techni-
cal philosophy. Instead of broadening philosophy, he
broadened aesthetics to include the most general ques-
tions of fundamental metaphysical presuppositions.

It has several times been remarked in the foregoing
that Schiller's arguments rest on at least two opposed
concepts of nature. Detailed analysis of all his philo-
sophical essays would reveal several intermediate
changes, but for our present purpose two will suffice
in illustration of the consequences for his theory of art
of these fundamentally different assumptions. As a
result of his first philosophical training in the Leibniz-
ian tradition, Schiller viewed nature as a rational sys-
tem: the picture of the world Leibniz furnishes is that
of a logically ordered structure to which human knowl-
edge aspires and to which it will ultimately corre-
spond. On this view, the validity of art lies in the
imitation of nature as the model of a rational system.
Art is valid only if representational and didactic, be-
cause it would be merely absurd and irrational to rep-
resent things other than they are. The subjective feel-
ings of the artist are relevant only to the extent that
they dimly reflect what is later found to be true—if
they do not, they are false and misleading. Schiller's

teachers, the books he was assigned to read, the cultural milieu in which he moved, the rigid discipline of the Academy he attended, the seemingly inflexible social structure, all combined to promote a subtle accord between the formalism of the rationalist position and his actual experience in those early years.

Contrast this view with that of *On the Sublime*. We cannot verify our concepts of nature against external reality and thus establish their truth. Hence the concepts we in fact entertain are products of our own creative imagination. If one is aware of this, a certain tension arises because the "objectivity" of the concepts must remain in doubt—nature as comprehended is possibly far removed from nature as it really is. If one is not aware of it, then one supposes an identity between "real" nature and nature as comprehended.

This is what Schiller finds in the naive poets. They have arrived at such a sense of identity unconsciously; yet so felicitous an outcome is denied to those unfortunately endowed with the wrong characteristics. These, the sentimental, are dominated by a longing for "objective" knowledge, and mistake the intuitive understanding of the naive for mere insensitivity and subjective complacency. Awareness is the operative word in the correction of these misunderstandings; and it is a function of aesthetic education to alert the individual of one type to the equal validity (and inadequacy) of the other type, so as to bring Schiller's ideal synthesis nearer to realization.

We find a parallel development in Schiller's epistemology, which likewise begins with rationalism and emerges by way of a notable encounter with Kant's theory of knowledge as the blend of conventionalism and idealism we are examining. The contrast between idealist and realist was drawn if only to show that neither position is tenable in isolation. When the attempt is pressed in either direction, the result is the fatalism of the realist and the fantasy of the idealist. Both positions suffer from the fallacy of supposing that a complete picture of reality can be supplied by their respective methods. Schiller draws out these contrasts at great length and, with Kant, agrees that human knowledge is objective in the sense that factual determinations, as universally agreed upon by all observers, are independent of the observers, and the uniformity of knowledge, as far as concerns its mere factualness, must be attributed to the uniformity of the object as it appears to the observers. Two kinds of uniformity are involved: the external object as it is given in appearance, and the uniformity of the human mind. So far Schiller agrees with Kant. The differences between them arise when one reaches the higher levels of cognition; in particular, when we are to account for the origin of explanatory hypotheses of great generality. No detailed analysis of Kant would be appropriate here, but the key point at issue must be brought out if we are to understand how Schiller introduces an aesthetic element, equated with freedom, into cognition and morality, in a way strikingly different from Kant's approach.

Kant's account of the synthetic a priori in the *Critique of Pure Reason* argues that there are elements in human knowledge, not themselves given in experience which, nonetheless, are the principles by which that knowledge must be ordered. As examples embodying these principles he cites Copernicus' astronomy, Newton's physics (B xxii), mathematics generally (B 14-18), Euclidian geometry in particular (B 64: "the

propositions of geometry . . . are known with apodeic-
tic certainty . . ."), and Aristotelian logic (B vii). All
of these Kant takes as true in the strict sense for human
reason (i.e., they can never be otherwise).

This is the point which Schiller seems to be disput-
ing. He rejects the supposition that these explanatory
theories are true in the strict sense. From what he says
about the nature of human knowledge it follows that
no explanations can ever be thought of as apodeicti-
cally certain in the sense advanced by Kant. As regu-
lative principles, these must be common to *all* human
beings; but the implications of Schiller's position deny
this. Different regulative principles are possible for
different temperamental types. It is precisely a conse-
quence of the rejection of Newton, Euclid, and Aris-
totle in certain very important respects in modern
science that led Poincaré and his school, for example,
to advance the suggestion that the axioms of these
systems are not the a priori certainties Kant asserts
them to be, but are true by convention. Schiller antici-
pates this position in those passages in the last half of
On the Sublime to which I have drawn attention. In
particular the remark that "nature has entered into no
compact with man" (XII 278, 34) and the express re-
jection of a "purposive bond" (276, 14) among the
appearances on which knowledge must be based lead
me to conclude that here Schiller is not only rejecting
the rationalists' need to find the world strictly ordered,
but is also rejecting those passages in Kant which
point to the purposiveness of nature as being neces-
sarily of a single kind.

There are two themes that emerge from this reac-
tion to Kant. The first is Schiller's argument in favor
of a plurality of human types against Kant's assertion

of a uniform human nature; this enables Schiller to break down the alleged uniformity of human knowledge from which Kant infers that synthetic a priori principles are universally binding on all human beings. The second theme, which I want to take up now, involves the consequences for human knowledge and freedom of Schiller's anticipations of the conventionalist position.

The world displays an order of some kind: Schiller concedes that the world is rational *in its totality* (XII 264, 6), though we may well question the precise ordering of any given event. This entitles us to exploit for their heuristic value the very general assumptions of simplicity, determinacy, and continuity in the world which we make even when we may not be entirely satisfied with our partial explanations. Nonetheless, even if we concede that the world is wholly determined in every respect, we still face the problem of saying what the laws are by which it is determined. It is a rationalist fallacy that Schiller has at last put firmly behind him to suppose that any of the laws we think we have discovered are necessarily true even for the limited range of phenomena from which they are derived:

> . . . the absolute impossibility of explaining *nature herself* by means of *natural laws,* and of imputing *to* her domain what holds *in* her domain . . . (278, 13)

Schiller thus finds a place for freedom and idealism in a world which, for all we know, may be wholly determinate. For, so long as the relation between the order of the noumenal world and that ordered body of laws which we impose upon the phenomenal is not a necessary one, it will not be possible to define truth and reality in terms either of a correspondence or a consistency theory. Schiller maintains that, so long as there is no prospect, even in principle, of verifying our laws against the noumenal world, we are free to formulate any theories whatever, provided that we accept the discipline of facts and logic. A further consequence, of the utmost importance for his aesthetic theory, is that, since the theories and laws are not themselves given, their formulation necessarily involves the aesthetic elements of imaginative creativity and the free exploitation of possibilities. While creativity in the elaboration of cognitive schemes must work within the limits of concrete fact, artistic creativity is concerned only with possibilities as such. Still, to avoid complete subjectivity and meaninglessness, an analogy with actual experience is needed. Schiller's critical concept here is *Schein*—semblance: illusion without delusion. Without the plausibility and conviction that bind aesthetic creation to experience it is merely fantastic. The status of the ideal as it concerns morality and the moral aspect of the art work is that in the art work freedom is manifested in a superlative degree. For here the limitations of empirical fact as they apply to cognition fall away, at least insofar as they apply to any actual state of events; and the mind is free to give expression to the highest aspirations of which it is capable. But it is important to stress that this form of idealism, so close to the conventional image of Schiller as poet, is never far removed from practical and factual considerations. No moral or aesthetic insight asserted in flagrant disregard of the facts of human experience can ever be warranted on the views Schiller advances.

I turn back now to the other theme referred to a little before—the rejection of Kant's view of the uniformity of human nature. A major contribution of Schiller's to the history of aesthetics and, loosely speaking, to philosophizing generally, is the typology of human nature. Jung devotes two lengthy chapters in his *Psychological Types* to Schiller's anticipations of his own psychological typology, notably the distinction between introvert and extravert. This is but another division among the many that have been offered. We are all familiar with Coleridge's dictum that everyone is born a little Platonist or a little Aristotelian, and with William James' division of thinkers into the tender- and tough-minded, the twice- and the once-born. One might add the contrast between classic and romantic, and Nietzsche's Apollonian and Dionysian types which spring directly from Schiller's influence. That there are such types is simply matter of fact; let us, by way of illustration consider another pair: the pessimist versus the optimist.

To the pessimist, human nature, if not fixed for all eternity, develops at an infinitesimal rate, and scarcely at all during the whole span of human history, such as it is. Depending on the view taken, this may be due to the commixture of matter with mind or soul, which in Kant becomes the source of "radical evil"; in Plato the ground of the impossibility that human knowledge can ever attain to the divine; in St. Augustine it is the reason for man's sinful condition and his dire dependence upon grace for salvation. Or, to leave the moral plane for the social, an analogous doctrine supplies an apology for the preservation of the status quo, as, for example, in Hobbes and Carlyle. Empiricists may as much be the victims of this view as rationalists, for it derives equally from the vitiating effects of a profound scepticism as to the foundations of human knowledge, as in Hume. Against this view, the argument is commonplace enough that here is a thinly disguised attempt to resist social change because the present arrangements suit those parties who have a vested interest in them. Mill offers such an objection in *Utilitarianism* against Kant and Carlyle.

To the optimist, the rational order of the world, if he is a rationalist, is of the same kind as human reason, and therefore can be apprehended; for an empiricist of one kind or another, that correspondence is imposed by human modes of cognition in such a way that it makes no sense to ask whether there is another "real" order which exists in the external world. However diverse the metaphysical points of view, all optimists agree that human problems are in principle soluble by human means; and the main objection to the pessimistic view is to the quietism and fatalism it often entails. If, as seems to follow from Schiller's argument, quarrels and misunderstandings between realists and idealists, optimists and pessimists, depend not on the facts, which are the same for both, but on attitudes; and if, further, philosophers have not concerned themselves with this question, but with special and onesided pleading in defense of their own uncritically accepted attitudes, then it is not surprising that he takes a sharply antiphilosophical tone as he pursues his defense of poetry. This is manifested all too clearly in his quarrel with Fichte, whom he accused of concealing a fundamental ignorance in graceless and obscure language.

In the last analysis the force of philosophical arguments will rest upon their empirico-logical coherence

and consistency only as necessary conditions depend-
ent in turn upon their psychological appeal as a suffi-
cient condition. The typological differences among
individuals will decide the choice among systematic
philosophies even for the most dispassionate of think-
ers. Anyone who cares to follow Schiller beyond this
point will see that the choice of any given philosophy,
because it must be made on temperamental grounds,
even though it may indeed serve a necessary function
as a heuristic device for practical purposes, is at the
same time bound to misrepresent the symbolic approxi-
mation which is the best that any such philosophy
can offer. The danger in philosophy lies in its tendency
to reify its concepts, to take the symbol for the thing
symbolized, to rest content with self-confirming and
circular propositions.

The damage that philosophy has suffered on this
analysis is of two kinds: first, there is the emphasis
that the choice of philosophy is decided by the indi-
vidual's psychological makeup rather than on any
possibly conclusive decision on the merits of the argu-
ments involved. Second, we have the conclusion that
technical philosophy is powerless to solve the funda-
mental metaphysical and epistemological questions.
The rationalist's confusion of logical validity with fac-
tual truth has its precise counterpart in the empiricist's
despair of finding any truth at all. The best alternative
to these views, as a practical matter, is the convention-
alist position which limits itself to defining certain
propositions as "true" by convention. There the con-
ventionalist stops with his network of interconnected
concepts and theoretical postulates dependent only
upon each other; but Schiller, as we shall see, goes on.
Philosophy, in the narrow sense in which it was prac-

tised in his day (i.e., to "convince universally"), is in
any case powerless to remedy the defects implicit in
its own methods. It remains for poetry, with its ex-
plicit renunciation of conceptual precision where none
is possible, to exploit the paradoxes of the insoluble
but inescapable problems of perennial human interest.
The theory of aesthetic education provides a solution
to the psychological issue as a corrective to an other-
wise irreducible typology; and the theory of aethetic
semblance (*Schein*) is addressed to the problem of
truth.

A Defense of Poetry

Schiller was aware of the famous passage in the *Re-
public* in which Plato challenged anyone who can
show the merit of poetry to justify the readmission of
the poets into the State. The issue there, as in Schiller,
centers upon the relation of poetry to truth. I now
want to argue that Schiller's late essays constitute a
defense in precisely the sense required.

Plato's attack on the poets in the *Republic* and *Ion*
is based upon the irrationality of the poetic impulse.
The poet utters he knows not what; he is enthused:
the god speaks through him (at best), but he can give
no unambiguous account of what he means; his words
are susceptible of varied and contradictory meanings
and interpretations, and his own interpretations are
not privileged. This criticism is fatal if either of two
conditions is satisfied: if poetry is a refuge from real-
ity, or if it is preferred to rational and ordered knowl-
edge. It is abundantly clear from our analysis of
Schiller's essays that he nowhere offers any support to

those who might seek in poetry the comforts of un-
reason, and this point needs no further elaboration.
The principal point at issue is the possibility of the
foundation of rational knowledge upon certain first
principles. In the discussion of the Divided Line (*Re-
public* V, 509D), Plato makes the developing structure
of human knowledge depend upon an ascending scale
of increasingly more general hypotheses; but he ap-
pears to overlook the logical status of any such hypoth-
eses. Where they are inductive, they cannot possess
any more certainty than the observations upon which
they rest—and no reader of Plato can be in any doubt
about how uncertain these must be! If "physics can
never be more than a likely story," the correspondence
theory of truth cannot yield any certainty, and one
must look instead to the consistency theory for a rem-
edy if one is to be found. But here Schiller is much
more explicit than Plato in his rejection of purely logi-
cal criteria for knowledge.

What then is the source of the hypotheses of great
generality by which the attempt is made to unify
knowledge? From the assumption that there is a truth
to be discovered, together with the invincible Greek
conviction that our reason can grasp it, Plato falls
back on the doctrine of *anamnesis* (recollection) as a
possible source for the kind of human knowledge
which cannot be found in mundane human experi-
ence. But the absolute certainty which *is* found, it is
clear from the *Meno,* is mathematical, that is to say, it
is logical, or more strictly, a tautological certainty. But
can one make any *necessary* inferences from logical
validity to factual truth? So long as Euclidian geome-
try, to take the most striking example, was believed to
rest on "axioms" which were necessarily true in the

world (as opposed to "postulates," which were acknowledged to be merely conventional), it was possible to maintain the necessary truth of the theorems derived within the system. From this assurance that some necessary truths could be discovered about the world, the whole rationalist position develops whereby the expectation seems plausible that if knowledge in any field can be ordered on the mathematical model, the same kind of certainty can be attained in that field, and eventually be extended to the whole range of human knowledge. Plotinus' and Leibniz' explicit assimilation of aesthetic to cognitive judgment is typical of this view. One need recall only Descartes' remarks in his *Discourse,* and Leibniz' hope of formulating a Universal Characteristic to solve everything, including ethical and political problems, to see how even the greatest minds could be misled by the astonishing coincidence of logic and experience in geometry. But this assurance was destroyed by Kant in metaphysics and epistemology, as we have seen. Schiller was among the earliest beneficiaries of the Kantian doctrine which, as he interpreted it, makes of human knowledge a strictly human affair. What has to be stressed in cognition is the *invention,* not the *discovery,* of laws and theories. This is where aesthetic insight comes into play.

If the general trend of this argument should now seem to lean toward a very substantial degree of subjectivity and arbitrariness in an area in which we expect the maximum of objectivity and certainty, then it must be conceded that this is just what Schiller is doing. The essay *On the Sublime* represents a most extraordinary *volte-face* in his thinking; so much so that it is a kind of "Copernican Revolution." His first efforts in aesthetics were all directed to showing, in opposition to Kant, that aesthetics is as objective as science; he failed in this, as he himself saw, for reasons that any modern reader would appreciate. But he goes on from the point at which most persons go off, muttering "de gustibus," to argue that, in certain critical respects, science is not more objective than aesthetics! To show this, he must pursue the attack on what is taken to be the most unshakable aspects of our knowledge. In speaking of the arbitrariness of the assumptions underlying scientific hypotheses it is, of course, understood that we are not free to presuppose absolutely anything, but are subject to the discipline of fact even more than of logic. It remains to show the role of the aesthetic impulse in cognition and in ethics, and that art as such is also subject to that same discipline of fact and logic.

There are criteria only for the definitive rejection of cognitive hypotheses; there are none for the conclusive acceptance of those which survive whatever empirical and logical tests can be brought to bear against them. The choice among hypotheses incompatible with each other but equally compatible with the facts is an aesthetic choice. It may be formulated in terms of criteria of simplicity, of the continuity and determinacy of natural processes, of the unity of the world; but these in turn rest upon an aesthetic predilection for the simple and the symmetrical over the complex and irregular. The aesthetic impulse is still more in evidence when one considers that there are no rules for the invention of hypotheses, and that theories of great generality are works of the imagination and of inventive genius entirely of the order of the greatest works of art. The vision displayed in, and the style of,

scientific invention, like those of the art work, will be
equally functions of the temperament of an individual
and of his age, operating either in harmony or in con-
flict, or, most rarely, with that indifference to the
ephemeral interests of his own age which so com-
pelled Schiller's fascinated admiration of Goethe.

We are thus led to identify within the structure of
cognitive processes an element which we can equate
in the broadest sense with the aesthetic impulse as it
likewise manifests itself in poetry. We may further
argue that without this aesthetic element in cognition
there would be no prospect of those hypotheses aris-
ing which, upon verification, are so fruitful in provid-
ing possible and even probable explanations of the
phenomena of experience.[20] In its relations to morality
the aesthetic impulse appears rather more ambigu-
ously, for Schiller does not go much beyond the Kant-
ian position, but we have earlier suggested that within
the framework even of Kant's rigorous formalism the
added breadth of aesthetic vision can readily be ac-
commodated. Art, especially drama, with its exem-
plary cases of moral dilemma, can expand the seeming
narrowness of some ethical positions (including Kant's)
by illuminating, as no technical exposition ever can,
the humanistic insight implicit in them.

The issue of truth, on this view, is represented in
the realm of aesthetic possibility by semblance; and
we should entertain toward our metaphysical postu-
lates an attitude of what Schiller calls "aesthetic play."
That is, our commitment toward what we assume real-
ity to be must represent a delicate balance: strong
enough to furnish sanction for action, but not so strong
as to harden into dogma. For, given the epistemologi-
cal premisses of Schiller's argument, no access to ab-

solute reality is possible; hence the flexibility of aesthetic play which requires a dynamic interaction of fact and imagination in order to redefine "reality" and "truth" in terms of the best formulations thus far available. Imagination is, however, much less limited where practical or pragmatic considerations are less immediate—there is room for man's reach to exceed his grasp—and poetry, by exploiting the "remote analogy" between an attained actuality and an ideal reality which can only be aspired to, will suggest within the capacity of an integral humanity the possible content of that ideal. Some will dwell on the disparity with melancholy; others will be exhilarated by the challenge of an intrinsic contradiction in human nature, but in either case the poetic vision, if cultivated, will expand the possible forms, and with them the actual content of human experience and knowledge.

Let us turn in conclusion to the role of aesthetic education and make explicit the points which underlie Schiller's defense of poetry. The function of aesthetic education is to render the individual sensitive to the uncertainty of human knowledge; it is instead to make him willing to surrender the need for a facile and misleading conception of truth, and reconcile him to the insoluble complexities of existence. It will stimulate him to rise above the leaden weight, not of facts, but of theories whose apparent fixity tends to discourage a vigorous activity on his part. By teaching him the mere relativity of the initial endowment of temperament, it relieves the shackling sense of determinism which vitiates the validity of the philosophical enterprise. In the sphere of morals and politics, as well as in religious beliefs, it destroys dogmatism and parochialism while leaving room for the passionate conviction which is never appropriate to matters of fact. In its emphasis upon the *possibility* of the truth of such convictions, the theory of aesthetic education concedes their indemonstrability and remains content with their irrefutability. The defense rests—the aesthetic impulse has been shown to be the indispensable condition of the expansion of human knowledge, of moral understanding, and of freedom.

SELECT BIBLIOGRAPHY

BASCH, VICTOR, *La Poétique de Schiller*. Paris: Alcan, 1902.

BAUMECKER, GOTTFRIED, *Schillers Schönheitslehre*. Heidelberg: Winter, 1937.

BESENBRUCH, WALTER, *Zum Problem des Typischen in der Kunst*. Weimar: Böhlau, 1956.

BOSANQUET, BERNARD, *A History of Aesthetic*. 2nd ed., London: Allen & Unwin, 1904.

DILTHEY, WILHELM, "Die Typen der Weltanschauung und ihre Ausbildung in den metaphysischen Systemen," in *Gesammelte Schriften*, Vol. 8. Ed. by B. Groethuysen. Stuttgart: Teubner; Göttingen: Vandenhoeck & Ruprecht, 1960, pp. 75-118.

ERMATINGER, EMIL, "Schillers weltanschauliche und aesthetische Auseinandersetzungen," in *Deutsche Dichter 1700-1900. Eine Geistesgeschichte in Lebensbildern*. Bonn: Athenäum, 1949, 57-78.

GAEDE, UDO, *Schillers Abhandlung "Über naive und sentimentalische Dichtung." Studien zur Entstehungsgeschichte*. Berlin: Duncker, 1899.

GERHARD, MELITTA, *Schiller*. Berne, Munich: Francke, 1950.

GROSSE, E., *Übersicht über Lessings Laokoon und Schillers Abhandlung über das Erhabene*. Berlin: Weidmann, 1902.

HARNACK, OTTO, *Schiller*. 2nd ed., Berlin: Hofmann, 1905.

JAMES, WILLIAM, *Pragmatism*. New York: Longmans, Green, 1907.

JUNG, CARL GUSTAV, *Psychological Types,* transl. by H. G. Baines. New Impression, London, Kegan, Paul, 1946.

KANT, IMMANUEL, *Critique of Judgment,* transl. by J. H. Bernard. New York: Hafner, 1951.

KÜHNEMANN, EUGEN, *Kants und Schillers Begründung der Aesthetik.* Munich: Beck, 1895.

MAINLAND, WILLIAM F. (ed.), *Schiller: Über naive und sentimentalische Dichtung.* Oxford: Blackwell, 1957.

MANN, THOMAS, *Versuch über Schiller. Seinem Andenken zum 150. Todestag in Liebe gewidmet.* Berlin, Frankfurt/M: Fischer, 1955.

MENG, HEINRICH, *Schillers Abhandlung über naive und sentimentalische Dichtung. Prolegomena zu einer Typologie des Dichterischen.* Frauenfeld, Leipzig: Huber, 1936.

SAINTSBURY, GEORGE, *A History of Criticism and Literary Taste in Europe.* Vol. 3: *Modern Criticism.* Edinburgh, London: Harrap, 1904.

Schillers Briefe, edited and annotated by Fritz Jonas. 7 volumes. Stuttgart: Deutsche Verlagsanstalt, 1892-96.

SOMMER, ROBERT, *Grundzüge einer Geschichte der deutschen Psychologie und Aesthetik.* Augsburg, 1892.

WALZEL, OSKAR, Introduction and Notes to Vols. XI and XII (Philosophical writings) of the *Säkular-Ausgabe.* Stuttgart, Berlin: Cotta, 1904-5.

WEIGAND, PAUL, "Psychological Types in Friedrich Schiller and William James," *Journal of the History of Ideas,* 13 (1952), pp. 376-83.

WIESE, BENNO VON, *Friedrich Schiller.* Stuttgart: Metzler, 1959.

NOTE ON THE TEXT

The text and pagination of the *Säkular-Ausgabe* (ed. Eduard von den Hellen, et al., Stuttgart and Berlin: Cotta, 1904-05) have been used throughout. References to Schiller's works are likewise to this edition.

Über naive und sentimentalische Dichtung originally appeared in three parts in successive issues of Schiller's journal *Die Horen:*

Über das Naive in No. 11 of 1795;

Die sentimentalischen Dichter in No. 12 of 1795;

Beschluss der Abhandlung über naive und sentimentalische Dichter, nebst einigen Bemerkungen einen charakteristischen Unterschied unter den Menschen betreffend in No. 1 of 1796.

Schiller's final redaction for publication in Vol. 2 of his *Kleinere prosaische Schriften* (1800) shows some changes, mainly the exclusion of topical references; but there are no particular textual problems, nor do the changes warrant special comment.

Über das Erhabene appeared first in Vol. 3 of the *Kleinere prosaische Schriften* (1801) without prior publication. This has given rise to controversy as to the date it was written, estimates ranging from 1793 to 1801. No conclusive evidence exists, but, as argued in the Introduction, in terms of the development of

Schiller's thought I favor the later date, at least for the latter half of the essay.

Schiller's footnotes are indicated by asterisks; the translator's are numbered. A few cross-headings, mostly indicating the original subdivisions of the text, have been supplied in brackets.

NAIVE AND
SENTIMENTAL POETRY

NAIVE AND SENTIMENTAL POETRY

[ON THE NAIVE (*Die Horen,* No. 11, 1795)]

(161) There are moments in our lives when we dedicate a kind of love and tender respect to nature in plants, minerals, animals, and landscapes, as well as to human nature in children, in the customs of country folk, and to the primitive world, not because it gratifies our senses, nor yet because it satisfies our understanding or taste (the very opposite can occur in both instances), rather, simply *because it is nature.* Every person of a finer cast who is not totally lacking in feeling experiences this when he wanders in the open air, when he stays in the country, or lingers before the monuments of ancient times; in short, whenever he is surprised in the midst of artificial circumstances and situations by the sight of simple nature. It is this interest, not infrequently elevated into a need, which underlies much of our fondness for flowers and animals, for simple gardens, for strolls, for the country and its inhabitants, for many an artifact of remote antiquity, and the like; provided that neither affectation nor any other fortuitous interest play a role. However, this kind of interest in nature can take place only under two conditions. First, it is absolutely necessary that the object which inspires it should be *nature* or at least be taken by us as such; [1] second, that it be *naive* (in the broadest meaning of

the word), i.e., that nature stand in contrast to art
and put it to shame. As soon as the latter (162) is
joined with the former, not before, nature becomes
naive.

Nature, considered in this wise, is for us nothing
but the voluntary presence, the subsistence of things
on their own, their existence in accordance with their
own immutable laws.

This representation is absolutely necessary if we
are to take an interest in such appearances. If one
were able by the most consummate deception to give
an artificial flower the similitude of nature, if one were
able to induce the highest illusion by imitation of the
naive in folk-customs, the discovery that it was imita-
tion would completely destroy the feeling of which
we spoke.* From this it is clear that this kind of
satisfaction in nature is not aesthetic but moral; for
it is mediated by an idea, not produced immediately
by observation; nor is it in any way dependent upon
beauty of form. For what could a modest flower, a
stream, a mossy stone, the chirping of birds, the hum-
ming of bees, etc., possess in themselves so pleasing
to us? What could give them a claim even upon our
love? It is not these objects, it is an idea represented

* Kant, who was the first, as far as I know, who began to re-
flect purposefully upon this phenomenon, remarks that if we
were to hear the song of the nightingale imitated with the
utmost deception by a human voice and had abandoned our-
selves to the impression with all our feelings, our entire delight
would disappear with the destruction of the illusion. See the
chapter on the intellectual interest in the beautiful in the *Cri-
tique of Aesthetic Judgment*. Anyone who has learned to ad-
mire the author only as a great thinker will be pleased here to
come upon a trace of his heart and be convinced by this dis-
covery of the man's high philosophical calling (which abso-
lutely requires the combination of both characteristics).

by them which we love in them. We love in them
the tacitly creative life (163), the serene spontaneity
of their activity, existence in accordance with their
own laws, the inner necessity, the eternal unity with
themselves.

They are what we were; they are what *we should
once again become.* We were nature just as they, and
our culture, by means of reason and freedom, should
lead us back to nature.[2] They are, therefore, not only
the representation of our lost childhood, which eter-
nally remains most dear to us, but fill us with a cer-
tain melancholy. But they are also representations of
our highest fulfilment in the ideal, thus evoking in us
a sublime tenderness.

Yet their perfection is not to their credit, because it
is not the product of their choice. They accord us
then, the quite unique delight of being our example
without putting us to shame. They surround us like a
continuous divine phenomenon, but more exhilarating
than blinding. What determines their character is pre-
cisely what is lacking for the perfection of our own;
what distinguishes us from them, is precisely what
they themselves lack for divinity. We are free, they
are necessary; we change, they remain a unity. But
only if both are joined one with the other—if the will
freely obeys the law of necessity, and reason asserts
its rule through all the flux of imagination, does the
ideal or the divine come to the fore. *In them,* then,
we see eternally that which escapes us, but for which
we are challenged to strive, and which, even if we
never attain to it, we may still hope to approach in
endless progress. *In ourselves* we observe an advan-
tage which they lack, and in which they can either
never participate at all (as in the case of the irra-

tional) or only insofar as they proceed by *our* path
(as with childhood). They afford us, therefore, the
sweetest enjoyment of our humanity as idea, even
though they must perforce humiliate us with reference
to any particular condition of our humanity.

(164)   Since this interest in nature is based upon
an idea, it can manifest itself only in minds which are
receptive to ideas, i.e., in moral minds. By far the ma-
jority of people merely affect this state, and the uni-
versality of this sentimental taste in our times as ex-
pressed, particularly since the appearance of certain
writings,[3] in the form of sentimental journeys, pleas-
ure gardens, walks, and other delights of this sort, is
by no means a proof of the universality of this mode
of feeling. Yet nature will always have something of
this effect even upon the most unfeeling, if only be-
cause that tendency toward the moral common to all
men is sufficient for the purpose, and we are all with-
out distinction, regardless of the distance between our
actions and the simplicity and truth of nature, im-
pelled to it in idea. Particularly powerfully and most
universally this sensitivity to nature is given expres-
sion at the instance of such objects as stand in close
connection with us, affording a retrospective view of
ourselves and revealing more closely the unnatural in
us, as, for example, in children and childlike folk. One
is in error to suppose that it is only the notion of
helplessness which overcomes us with tenderness at
certain moments when we are together with children.
That may perhaps be the case with those who in the
presence of weakness are accustomed only to feeling
their own superiority. But the feeling of which I speak
(it occurs only in specifically moral moods and is not
to be confused with the emotion that is excited in us

by the happy activity of children) is humiliating rather than favorable to self-love; and even if an advantage were to be drawn from it, this would certainly not be on our side. We are touched not because we look down upon the child from the height of our strength and perfection, but rather because we *look upward* from the *limitation* of our condition, which is inseparable from the *determination* which we have attained, to the unlimited *determinacy* [4] (165) of the child and to its pure innocence; and our emotion at such a moment is too transparently mixed with a certain melancholy for its source to be mistaken. In the child *disposition* and *determination* are represented; in us that *fulfilment* that forever remains far short of those. The child is therefore a lively representation to us of the ideal, not indeed as it is fulfilled, but as it is enjoined; hence we are in no sense moved by the notion of its poverty and limitation, but rather by the opposite: the notion of its pure and free strength, its integrity, its eternality. To a moral and sensitive person a child will be a *sacred* object on this account; an object, in fact, which by the greatness of an idea destroys all empirical greatness; one which, whatever else it may lose in the judgment of the understanding, it regains in ample measure in the judgment of reason.

It is from just this contradiction between the judgment of reason and the understanding that the quite extraordinary phenomenon arises of those mixed feelings which the *naive* mode of thought excites in us. It connects *childlike* simplicity with the *childish;* through the latter it exposes its weakness to the understanding and causes that smile by which we betray our (*theoretical*) superiority. But as soon as we have cause to

believe that childish simplicity is at the same time
childlike, that in consequence not lack of understand-
ing, not incapacity, but rather a higher (*practical* [5])
strength, a heart full of innocence and truth, is the
source of that which out of its inner greatness scorns
the aid of art, then that triumph of the understanding
is set aside, and mockery of ingenuousness yields to
admiration of simplicity. We feel ourselves obliged to
respect the object at which we formerly smiled, and
since we at the same time cast our glance upon our-
selves, bemoan the fact that we are not likewise
endowed. Thus arises (166) the entirely unique phe-
nomenon of a feeling in which joyous mockery, re-
spect, and melancholy are compounded.*

---

* In a note appended to the Analytic of the Sublime (*Critique
of Aesthetic Judgment,* p. 225, 1st edition) Kant likewise dis-
tinguishes these threefold ingredients in the feeling of the
naive, but he supplies another explanation. "Something com-
pounded of both (the animal feeling of pleasure and the spiri-
tual feeling of respect) is found in naivety, which is the burst-
ing forth of that sincerity originally natural to mankind in
opposition to the art of dissimulation that has become second
nature. We laugh at a simplicity that does not yet understand
how to conceal itself, yet we are delighted at the simplicity of
nature which here thwarts that art. We expected some routine
mode of utterance, artificial and carefully contrived to make a
fine impression, and yet we see unspoiled innocent nature
which we no more expected to see than he who displayed it
intended it to be exposed. That the fair but false impression
which ordinarily weighs so much in our judgment is now sud-
denly transformed into nothing—that the scoundrel in us, as it
were, is revealed—sets the mind in motion in two opposed
directions one after the other, giving the body a salutary
shock. A mixture of solemnity and high esteem appears in this
play of the faculty of judgment, because something infinitely
superior to all conventional manners, namely, purity of thought
(or at least an inclination thereto) is, after all, not wholly extin-
guished in human nature. But since it appears only fleetingly

To be naive it is necessary that (167) nature be victorious over art,* whether this occur counter to the knowledge or will of the individual or with his full awareness. In the first case this is the naive of *surprise* and amuses us; in the second, it is the naive *temperament* and touches us.

With the naive of surprise the individual must be

---

* Perhaps I should say quite briefly: *truth victorious over deceit;* but the concept of the naive seems to me still more inclusive, since any form of simplicity that triumphs over artifice, and natural freedom over stiffness and constraint, excites a similar emotion in us.

---

and the art of dissimulation swiftly draws a veil before it, there is at the same time an admixture of regret, which is an emotion of tenderness; an emotion which, taken as a joke, is very easily combined with good-humored laughter (and in fact is usually so combined), and which simultaneously compensates for the embarrassment of whoever gave rise to the occasion for not yet being experienced in the ways of men."—I confess that this mode of explanation does not entirely satisfy me, and this principally because it asserts of the naive as a whole what is at most true only of a species of it, the (167) naive of surprise, of which I shall speak later. It certainly arouses laughter if somebody exposes himself by naivety, and in some cases this laughter may derive from a preceding expectation that fails to materialize. But even naivety of the noblest sort, the naive of temperament, arouses a smile always, which however is scarcely due to any expectation that comes to nothing, but that can only be explained by the contrast between certain behavior and the conventionally accepted and expected forms. I doubt also whether the regret which is mingled in our feeling about the latter kind of naivety refers to the naive person and not rather to ourselves or to humanity at large, whose decay we are reminded of in such cases. It is too clearly a moral regret which must have some nobler object than the physical ills by which sincerity is threatened in the ordinary course of things, and this object can hardly be any other than the loss of truth and simplicity in mankind.

morally capable of denying nature; with the naive
temperament this may not be the case, but we must
not be able to think him *physically* incapable of doing
so if it is to affect us as being naive. The actions and
speech of children thus give us a pure impression of
the naive only so long as we do not recall their in-
capacity for art and in any case only (168) take into
consideration the contrast between their naturalness
and the artificiality in ourselves. The naive is *child-
likeness where it is no longer expected,* and precisely
on this account cannot be ascribed to actual childhood
in the most rigorous sense.

But in both cases, in the naive of surprise just as in
the naive of temperament, nature must be in the right
where art is in the wrong.

Only by this last provision is the concept of the
naive completed. The affect [6] is also nature, and the
rule of propriety is something artificial; yet the vic-
tory of the affect over propriety is anything but naive.
If, on the other hand, the same affect should triumph
over artifice, over false modesty, over deceit, then we
do not hesitate to call it naive.* Hence it is necessary

---

* A child is badly behaved if, out of greediness, foolhardiness,
or impetuosity, it acts in opposition to the prescripts of a good
education, but it is naive if its free and healthy nature rids it
of the mannerisms of an irrational education, such as the awk-
ward posturings of the dancing master. The same occurs with
the naive in its wholly figurative meaning, when it is trans-
ferred from the human to the inanimate. Nobody would find
naive the spectacle of a badly tended garden in which the
weeds have the upper hand, but there is certainly something
naive when the free growth of spreading branches undoes the
painstaking work of the topiarist in a French garden. Likewise,
it is in no way naive if a trained horse performs its lessons
badly out of natural stupidity, but something of the naive is
present if it forgets them out of natural freedom.

that nature should triumph over art not by her blind
violence as *dynamic greatness,* but by her form as
moral greatness, in brief, not as *compulsion,* but as
inner necessity. It is not the inadequacy of art but
its invalidity that must have assured the victory of
nature; for inadequacy is (169) a shortcoming, and
nothing that derives from a shortcoming can inspire
respect. It is indeed the case with the naive of sur-
prise that the superior power of the affect and a lack
of awareness reveal nature; but this lack and the su-
perior power by no means constitute the naive, rather
they simply provide the opportunity for nature to
obey unimpeded her moral character, i.e., the law of
harmony.

The naive of surprise can apply only to a human
being, and then only insofar as in this moment he is no
longer pure and innocent nature. It presupposes a will
that is not in harmony with nature's own acts. Such a
person, when brought to awareness, will take fright at
himself; the naive *temperament,* on the other hand,
will marvel at people and at their astonishment. But
since, in the naive of surprise, the truth is revealed not
by the personal and moral character, but by the nat-
ural character as revealed through the affect, we can-
not attribute any merit to the individual for his sin-
cerity, and our laughter is mockery deserved, which
will not be restrained by any personal esteem for the
individual. But since even in this case it is the sincer-
ity of nature that breaks through the veil of falsity, a
satisfaction of a higher order will be joined with the
malicious joy at having caught somebody out; for na-
ture in contrast with deceit must always engender
respect. We therefore experience a truly moral pleas-

ure even at the expense of the naive of surprise, al-
though not at the expense of moral character.*

(170) In the naive of surprise we do indeed always
respect nature because we are obliged to respect truth;
in the naive of temperament, on the other hand, we
respect the person and hence enjoy not only a moral
pleasure but a moral object. In both cases nature is in
the *right* in that it speaks truth; but in the latter case
not only is nature in the right, but the individual also
possesses *honor*. In the first case the sincerity of nature
accrues to the shame of the individual because it is
involuntary; in the second it always accrues to his
credit, provided of course that whatever he said would
otherwise have put him to shame.

We ascribe a naive temperament to a person if he,
in his judgment of things, overlooks their artificial and
contrived aspects and heeds only their simple nature.
We demand of him whatever can be judged about
things within healthy nature, and absolutely ignore
whatever presupposes any detachment from nature

* Since the naive depends solely on the manner in which some-
thing is said or done, this characteristic disappears from view
as soon as the matter itself assumes a predominant (170) or
even contradictory impression either by its causes or its effects.
Naivety of this kind can even disclose a crime, but then we
have neither the calm nor the time to direct our attention to
the form of the disclosure, and revulsion at the personal char-
acter swallows up our pleasure in the natural character. Just as
our outraged feelings deprive us of moral delight in the sin-
cerity of nature when we discover a crime as a result of naivety,
so also the compassion excited destroys our malicious joy when
we witness someone endangered by his naivety.
[Translator's note: the references to disclosure of a crime ap-
pear to anticipate Schiller's poem of 1797, *Die Kraniche des
Ibykus,* in which a pair of murderers betray themselves because
they see in the cranes flying overhead an omen of the pursu-
ing Furies.]

whether due to thought or feeling, or if at all affected
by them.

If a father tells his child that some man or other is
expiring from poverty, and the child goes and gives the
poor man his father's purse, such an action is naive;
for healthy nature is acting through the child, and in a
world in which (171) healthy nature were predomi-
nant he would be entirely right to act so. He sees only
the distress and the means nearest at hand to alleviate
it; such a development of property rights as permits a
portion of humanity to perish has no basis in simple
nature. The child's act, therefore, puts the world to
shame, and this our hearts also confess by the satisfac-
tion they derive from such an act.

If a man without knowledge of the world, but other-
wise sound of understanding, tells his secrets to an-
other who is deceiving him, but who is able skillfully
to conceal his motives and so, by his own sincerity,
lends the other the means with which to harm him,
this we find naive. We laugh at him, yet we cannot
refrain from esteeming him. For his trust in the other
man springs from the uprightness of his own tempera-
ment; at least he is naive only insofar as this is the
case.[7]

The naive mode of thought can therefore never be
a characteristic of depraved men, rather it can be at-
tributed only to children and to those of a childlike
temperament. These latter often act and think naively
in the midst of the artificial circumstances of fashion-
able society; they forget in their own beautiful human-
ity that they have to do with a depraved world, and
comport themselves even at the courts of kings with
the same ingenuousness and innocence that one would
find only in a pastoral society.

It is, incidentally, not at all easy to distinguish always between childish and childlike innocence, since there are actions which hover on the extreme boundary between both, and where we are left absolutely in doubt whether we should laugh at their simplemindedness or esteem their simplicity. There is a very remarkable example of this type in the history of the reign of Pope Hadrian VI [8] which has been described for us by Herr Schröckh with his customary punctiliousness and factual accuracy. This (172) Pope, a Dutchman by birth, occupied the Holy See at one of the most critical times for the hierarchy, when an embittered faction was exposing the shortcomings of the Roman Church without mercy, and the opposing faction was interested in the highest degree in concealing them. What the truly naive character, if indeed such a one should ever stray upon the seat of St. Peter, should have done in this case, is not the question; rather, it is how far such naivety of temperament might be compatible with the role of the Pope. This it was, however, that placed the predecessors and successors of Hadrian in the extremest embarrassment. They uniformly followed the established Roman system of making no admissions whatever. But Hadrian truly possessed the upright character of his nation and the innocence of his former station. From the narrow sphere of the scholar he was translated to his supreme position, and even upon the heights of his new office had not become untrue to that simple character. The abuses in the Church disturbed him, and he was far too straightforward to dissimulate publicly what he privately admitted to himself. In accordance with this manner of thinking he allowed himself in the instructions he sent with his legate to Germany to be betrayed into admissions which had never been heard of from any Pope, and which ran directly counter to the principles of this Court. "We well know," they read in part, "that for many years much that is abominable has issued from this Holy See; no wonder, then, if the diseased condition has been transmitted from the head to the limbs, from the Pope to the prelates. We have all fallen by the way, and it has already been long since one of us has done any good thing, not even one." Elsewhere he instructs the legate to declare in his name that he, Hadrian, was not to be blamed for anything that has been done by the popes before him, and that such excesses, even when he was still living in a lowly estate, had always displeased (173) him, and so forth. One can easily imagine how such naivety on the part of the Pope must have been received by the Roman clergy; the least that was laid to his charge was that he had betrayed the Church to the heretics. This most impolitic measure by the Pope would, nevertheless, be worthy of our entire respect and admiration, if we could only convince ourselves that he was really naive, that is, that it had been elicited from him solely by the natural candor of his character without any consideration for the possible consequences, and that he would have done no less had he been aware of the whole extent of the imprudence involved. But we have some reason to believe that he took this course to be by no means so impolitic, and went so far in his innocence as to hope by his complaisance to have won from his adversaries something very important to the advantage of his Church. He not only imagined that as a man of honor he was obliged to take this step, but also he could justify it as Pope; but, since he forgot that the most artificial of all institutions could be maintained only by a continued denial of the truth, he committed the inexcusable error of applying rules of conduct which might have proven correct under natural circumstances in an entirely opposite situation. This perforce much alters our judgment; and even if we cannot withhold our respect for the uprightness of the heart from which that action flowed, yet it is not a little diminished by the consideration that here nature had too weak an opponent in art, and the heart in the head.

Every true genius must be naive, or it is not genius. Only its naivety makes for its genius, and what it is intellectually and aesthetically it cannot disavow morally. Unacquainted with the rules, those crutches for weakness and taskmasters of awkwardness, led only by nature or by instinct, its guardian angel, it goes calmly and (174) surely through all the snares of false taste in which, if it is not shrewd enough to avoid them from afar, the nongenius must inevitably be entrapped. Only to genius is it given to be at home beyond the accustomed and to *extend* nature without *going beyond* her. It is true that sometimes the latter befalls even the greatest geniuses, but only because even they have their moments of fantasy in which protective nature abandons them either because they are engrossed by the power of example, or because the perverted taste of their times misleads them.

The genius must solve the most complex tasks with unpretentious simplicity and facility; the egg of Columbus appears in every decision of genius. And only thus does genius identify itself as such, by triumphing over the complications of art by simplicity. It proceeds not by the accepted principles, but by flashes of insight and feeling; but its insights are the inspirations of a god (everything done by healthy nature is divine), its feelings are laws for all ages and for all races of men.

The childlike character that the genius imposes upon his works he likewise displays in his private life and morals. He is *chaste*, for this nature always is; but he is not *prudish*, for only decadence is prudish. He is *intelligent*, for nature can never be otherwise; but he is not *cunning*, for only art can be so. He is *true* to his character and his inclinations, but not so much because he possesses principles as because nature, despite all fluctuations, always returns to its former state, always revives the old necessity. He is *modest*, even shy, because genius always remains a mystery to itself; but he is not fearful, because he does not know the dangers of the path he travels. We know little of the private lives of the greatest geniuses, but even the little that is preserved, for example, of Sophocles, Archimedes, Hippocrates, and, in more recent times, (175) of Ariosto, Dante, and Tasso, of Raphael, of Albrecht Dürer, Cervantes, Shakespeare, of Fielding, Sterne, etc., confirms this assertion.

Indeed, and this seems to present much more difficulty, even great statesmen and generals, if their greatness is due to their genius, will display a naive character. Among the ancients I cite only Epaminondas and Julius Caesar, among moderns only Henri IV of France, Gustavus Adolphus of Sweden, and Czar Peter the Great. The Duke of Marlborough, Turenne, and Vendôme all display this character. It is to the opposite sex that nature has assigned the naive character in its highest perfection. Woman's desire to please manifests itself nowhere so much as in seeking the *appearance of naivety*; proof enough, even if one had no other, that the greatest power of the sex depends upon this characteristic. But since the leading principles of feminine education are in perpetual conflict with this character, it is as difficult for a woman morally as it is for a man intellectually to preserve this magnificent gift of nature intact along with the advantages of a good education; and the *woman* who combines naivety of manner with a demeanor appropriate for society, is as worthy of the highest esteem as the scholar who joins the genius' freedom of thought with all the rigors of the schools.

From the naive mode of thought there necessarily follows naive expression in word as well as in gesture, and this is the most important element in gracefulness. By this naive grace genius expresses its most sublime and profound thought; the utterances of a god in the mouth of a child. The understanding of the schools, always fearful of error, crucifies its words and its concepts upon the cross of grammar and logic, and is severe and stiff to avoid uncertainty at all costs, employs many words to be quite sure of not saying too much, and deprives its thoughts of their strength and edge (176) so that they may not cut the unwary.[9] But genius delineates its own thoughts at a single felicitous stroke of the brush with an eternally determined, firm, and yet absolutely free outline. If to the former the sign remains forever heterogeneous and alien to the thing signified, to the latter language springs as by some inner necessity out of thought, and is so at one with it that even beneath the corporeal frame the spirit appears as if laid bare. It is precisely this mode of expression in which the sign disappears completely in the thing signified, and in which language, while giving expression to a thought, yet leaves it exposed where otherwise it cannot be represented without simultaneously concealing it; and this it is we generally call a gifted style displaying genius.[10]

As freely and naturally as genius expresses itself in its works of the spirit, its innocence of heart is expressed in its social intercourse. Because we have fallen to the same degree as far short from simplicity and strict truth of expression in life in society as from simplicity of temperament, our easily wounded guilt, as well as our easily seduced powers of imagination, have made a timid propriety necessary. Without being false, one often speaks otherwise than one thinks; one is forced into periphrasis in order to say things which could cause pain only to a sick egotism or danger to a perverted fantasy. Ignorance of these conventional rules combined with natural sincerity that despises every crumb and trace of falsity (not crudity, which it ignores as offensive), produces a naivety of expression in society that consists of calling things which one may mention either only in some artificial manner, or not at all, by their true names and in the most succinct fashion. Of this sort are the customary expressions of children. They arouse laughter by their contrast with the usages, but one must always confess in one's heart that the child is right.

(177) The naive temperament, strictly speaking, can indeed be ascribed only to the human being as a being not absolutely subject to nature, even though only insofar as pure nature actually still is active within him; but by an effect of the poetaster's imagination it is often transferred from the rational to the irrational. Thus we often attribute a naive character to an animal, a landscape, a building, even to nature in general, in opposition to the caprice and the fantastic concepts of

men. But this always demands that we assign a will to
the involuntary in our thoughts and insist on its rigor-
ous consequence according to the law of necessity. The
dissatisfaction at our own badly abused moral freedom
and at the moral harmony we sense is lacking in our
actions easily induces a mood in which we address the
irrational as a person, making a virtue of its eternal
uniformity, and envying its calm bearing, as though
there were really some temptation to be otherwise
which it had resisted. At such a moment it suits us
well to take the prerogative of our reason as a curse
and an evil and, in our lively apprehension of the im-
perfection of our actual performance, lose sight of the
economy of our predisposition and determination.

Then we see in irrational nature only a happier sister
who remained in our mother's house, out of which we
impetuously fled abroad in the arrogance of our free-
dom. With painful nostalgia we yearn to return as soon
as we have begun to experience the pressure of civili-
zation and hear in the remote lands of art our mother's
tender voice. As long as we were children of nature
merely, we enjoyed happiness and perfection; we be-
came free, and lost both. Thence arises a dual and
very unequal longing for nature, (178) a longing for
her *happiness,* a longing for her *perfection.* The sensu-
ous man bemoans the loss of the first; only the moral
man can grieve at the loss of the other.

Then ask of yourself, sensitive friend of nature,
whether your lassitude craves her peace, your injured
morality her harmony? Ask yourself, when art revolts
you and the abuses in society drive you to lifeless na-
ture in loneliness, whether it is society's deprivations,
its burdens, its tedium, or whether it is its moral an-
archy, its arbitrariness, its disorders that you despise in

it? In the former your courage must joyfully rush in, and the substitute you offer must be the freedom whence they derive. You may indeed retain the calm happiness of nature as your distant object, but only as one which is the reward of your worthiness. Then no more of complaints at the difficulties of life, of the inequality of stations, of the pressure of circumstances, of the uncertainty of possession, of ingratitude, oppression, persecution; with free resignation, you must subject yourself to all the *ills* of civilization, respect them as the natural conditions of the only good; only its *evil* you must mourn, but not with vain tears alone. Rather, take heed that beneath that mire you remain pure, beneath that serfdom, free; constant in that capricious flux, acting lawfully in that anarchy. Be not afraid of the confusion around you, only of the confusion within you; strive after unity, but do not seek conformity; strive after calm, but through harmony, not through the cessation of your activity. That nature which you envy in the irrational is worthy of no respect, no longing. It lies behind you, and must lie eternally behind you. Abandoned by the ladder that supported you, no other choice now lies open to you, but with free consciousness and will to grasp the law, or fall without hope of rescue into a bottomless pit.

(179) But when you are consoled at the lost *happiness* of nature then let her *perfection* be your heart's example. If you march out toward her from your artificial environment she will stand before you in her great calm, in her naive beauty, in her childlike innocence and simplicity—then linger at this image, cultivate this emotion; this is worthy of your sublimest humanity. Let it no longer occur to you to want to exchange with her, but take her up within yourself

and strive to wed her eternal advantage with your eternal prerogative,[11] and from both produce the divine. Let her surround you like an enchanting idyll in which you can always find yourself safe from the waywardness of art, and in which you accumulate courage and new confidence for the race, and which lights anew in your heart the flame of the ideal which is so easily extinguished in the storms of life.

If one recalls the beautiful nature that surrounded the ancient Greeks; if one ponders how familiarly this people could live with free nature beneath their fortunate skies, how very much closer their mode of conception, their manner of perception, their morals, were to simple nature, and what a faithful copy of this their poetry is, then the observation must be displeasing that one finds so little trace among them of the *sentimental* interest with which we moderns are attached to the scenes and characters of nature. The Greek is indeed to the highest degree precise, faithful, and circumstantial in describing them, yet simply no more so and with no more preferential involvement of his heart than he displays in the description of a tunic, a shield, a suit of armor, some domestic article, or any mechanical product. In his love of an object, he does not seem to make any distinction between those which appear of themselves, and those which arise as a result of art or the human will. Nature seems to interest his understanding and craving for knowledge more than his moral feeling; he (180) does not cling to her with fervor, with sentimentality, with sweet melancholy, as we moderns do. Indeed, by hypostatizing nature's individual phenomena, treating them as gods, and their effects as the acts of free beings, the Greek eliminates that calm necessity of nature precisely in virtue of which she is so attractive to us. His impatient fantasy leads him beyond nature to the drama of human life. Only the live and free, only characters, acts, destinies, and customs satisfy him, and if *we*, in certain moral moods of the mind, might wish to surrender the advantage of our freedom of will, which exposes us to so much conflict within ourselves, to so much unrest and errant bypaths, to the choiceless but calm necessity of the irrational, the fantasy of the Greek, in direct opposition to this, is engaged in rooting human nature in the inanimate world and assigning influence to the will where blind necessity reigns.

Whence derive these different spirits? How is it that we, who are in everything which is nature so boundlessly inferior to the ancients, offer tribute to nature just in this regard to such a higher degree, cling to her with fervor, and embrace even the inanimate world with the warmest sensibility? It is *because* nature in us has disappeared from humanity and we rediscover her in her truth only outside it, in the inanimate world. Not in our greater *accord with nature,* but quite the contrary, the *unnaturalness* of our situation, conditions, and moods forces us to procure a satisfaction in the physical world, since none is to be hoped for in the moral; for the incipient impulse for truth and simplicity which, like the moral tendency whence it derives, lies incorruptible and inalienable in every human heart. For this reason the feeling by which we are attached to nature is so closely related to the feeling with which we mourn the lost age of childhood (181) and childlike innocence. Our childhood is the only undisfigured nature that we still encounter in civilized mankind, hence it is no wonder if every trace of the nature outside us leads us back to our childhood.

It was quite otherwise with the ancient Greeks.*
With them civilization did not manifest itself to such
an extent that nature was abandoned in consequence.
The whole structure of their social life was founded on
perceptions, not on a contrivance of art; their theology
itself was the inspiration of a naive feeling, the child
of a joyous imaginative power, not of grovelling rea-
son like the church beliefs of modern nations; since,
then, the Greek had not lost nature in his humanity, he
could not be surprised by her outside it either and
thus feel a pressing need for objects in which he might
find her again. At one with himself and happy in the
sense of his humanity he was obliged to remain with it
as his maximum and assimilate all else to it; whereas
we, not at one with ourselves and unhappy (182) in
our experience of mankind, possess no more urgent in-
terest than to escape from it and cast from our view so
unsuccessful a form.

* But also only with the Greeks; since just such an active mo-
tion and such a rich fullness of human life as surrounded the
Greeks was required to breathe life even into the lifeless and
to pursue the image of humanity with this avidity. For example,
the world peopled by Ossian was shabby and uniform; the
inanimate world that surrounded it, however, was broad, colos-
sal and powerful, so it imposed itself and asserted its rights
even over the people. In the songs of this poet, therefore,
inanimate nature (in contrast with the people) figures much
more than as an object of perception. Yet even Ossian com-
plains of a decline of humanity and, as small among his
people as the extent of civilization and its perversions was, yet
the awareness of it was still lively and penetrating enough to
drive the emotion-laden moral poet back to the inanimate and
to pour out in his songs that elegiac tone that makes them so
moving and attractive to us.
[Translator's note: Ossian, the alleged 3rd-century Irish author
of epic poems by James Macpherson (1765). Schiller's observa-
tion of the sentimental tone confirms his argument, even
though he seems unaware of the forgery.]

The feeling of which we here speak is therefore not that which the ancients possessed; it is rather identical with that which *we have for the ancients*. They felt naturally; we feel the natural. Without a doubt the feeling that filled Homer's soul as he made his divine swineherd regale Ulysses was quite different from that which moved young Werther's soul as he read this song after an irritating evening in society. Our feeling for nature is like the feeling of an invalid for health.

Just as nature began gradually to disappear from human life as *experience* and as the (active and perceiving) *subject,* so we see her arise in the world of poetry as *idea* and *object*. The nation that had brought this to the extremest degree both in the unnatural and in reflection thereon must have been first to be most moved by the phenomenon of the naive and gave it a name. This nation was, as far as I know, the French. But the feeling of the naive and interest in it is naturally much older and goes back even before the beginning of moral and aesthetic corruption. This change in the mode of perception is, for example, extremely obvious in Euripides, if one compares him with his predecessors, notably with Aeschylus, and yet the later poet was the favorite of his age. The same revolution can likewise be documented among the old historians. Horace, the poet of a cultivated and corrupt era, praises serene happiness in Tibur, and one could call him the founder of this sentimental mode of poetry as well as a still unexcelled model of it. In Propertius, too, and Vergil, among others, one finds traces of this mode of perception, less so in (183) Ovid, in whom the requisite fullness of heart was lacking and who in exile in Tomi painfully missed the happiness that Horace in Tibur so gladly dispensed with.

The poets are everywhere, as their very name suggests, the *guardians* of nature. Where they can no longer quite be so and have already felt within themselves the destructive influence of arbitrary and artificial forms or have had to struggle with them, then they will appear as the *witnesses* and *avengers* of nature. They will either *be* nature, or they will *seek* lost nature. From this arises two entirely different modes of poetry which, between them, exhaust and divide the whole range of poetry. All poets who are truly so will belong, according to the temper of the times in which they flourish, or according to the influence upon their general education or passing states of mind by fortuitous circumstances, either to the *naive* or to the *sentimental* poets.

The poet of a naive and bright youthful world, like the poet who in ages of artificial civilization is closest to him, is severe and modest like virginal Diana in her forests; without intimacy he flees the heart that seeks his, flees the desire that would embrace him. The dry truth with which he deals with the object seems not infrequently like insensitivity.[12] The object possesses him entirely, his heart does not lie like a tawdry alloy immediately beneath the surface, but like gold waits to be sought in the depths. Like divinity behind the world's structure he stands behind his work; *he* is the work, and the work is *he;* to ask only for *him* is not to be worthy of it, inadequate to it, or sated with it.

Thus, for example, Homer among the ancients and Shakespeare among the moderns reveal themselves; two vastly different natures separated by the immeasurable distance of the years, but *one* in precisely this trait of character. (184) When, at a very early age I first made the acquaintance of the latter poet, I was

incensed by his coldness, the insensitivity which per-
mitted him to jest in the midst of the highest pathos,
to interrupt the heartrending scenes in *Hamlet*, in *King
Lear*, in *Macbeth*, etc., with a Fool; restraining himself
now where my sympathies rushed on, then coldblood-
edly tearing himself away where my heart would have
gladly lingered. Misled by acquaintance with more
recent poets into looking first for the poet in his work,
to find *his* heart, to reflect in unison with *him* on his
subject matter, in short, to observe the object in the
subject, it was intolerable to me that here there was no
way to lay hold of the poet, and nowhere to confront
him. I studied him and he possessed my complete ad-
miration for many years before I learned to love him
as an individual. I was not yet prepared to understand
nature at first hand. I could only support her image
reflected in understanding and regulated by a rule,
and for this purpose the sentimental poets of the
French, and the Germans, too, of the period from 1750
to about 1780, were just the right subjects. However, I
am not ashamed of this youthful judgment, since the
old-established criticism had promulgated a similar
one and was naive enough to publish it in the world.[13]

The same occurred to me with Homer also, whom I
learned to know only at a later period. I recall now the
curious point in the sixth book of the *Iliad* where
Glaucus and Diomedes come face to face in the battle
and, having recognized one another as guest-friends,
afterwards exchange gifts. This touching depiction of
the piety with which the rules of *hospitality* were ob-
served even in battle can be compared with an account
of the *knightly sense of nobility* in Ariosto, when two
knights and rivals, Ferraù and Rinaldo, the latter a
Christian, the former a Saracen, covered with wounds

after a violent duel, make peace and in order to over-
take the fleeing Angelica, (185) mount the same horse.
Both examples, as different as they may be otherwise,
are almost alike in their effect upon our hearts, because
both depict the beautiful victory of morals over pas-
sion and touch us by the naivety of their attitudes. But
how differently the poets react in describing these sim-
ilar actions. Ariosto, the citizen of a later world which
had fallen from simplicity of manners, cannot, in re-
counting the occurrence, conceal his own wonderment
and emotion. The feeling of the distance between those
morals and those which characterized his own age
overwhelms him. He abandons for a moment the por-
trait of the object and appears in his own person.[14]
This beautiful stanza is well known and has always
been greatly admired:

> O nobility of ancient knightly mode!
> Who once were rivals, divided still
> In godly faith, bitter pain still suffered,
> Bodies torn in enmity's wild struggle,
> Free of suspicion, together rode
> Along the darkling crooked path.
> The steed, by four spurs driven, sped
> To where the road in twain divided.*

And now old Homer! Scarcely has Diomedes learned
from the narrative of Glaucus, his antagonist, that the
latter's fathers were guest-friends of his deme, than he
thrusts his lance into the ground, speaks in a friendly
tone with him and agrees with him that in future they
will avoid one another in battle. Let us, however, hear
Homer himself:

* *Orlando Furioso*, First Canto, Stanza 22.

In me you will now have a good friend in Argos, and I shall have you in Lycia, if ever I visit that country. So let us avoid each other's spears, even in the melee, since there are plenty of the Trojans and their famous allies for me to kill, if I have the luck and speed to catch them, and plenty of Achaeans for you to slaughter, if you can. (186) And let us exchange our armor, so that everyone may know that our grandfathers' friendship has made friends of us. With no more said, they leapt from their chariots, shook hands, and pledged each other.

It would hardly be possible for a *modern* poet (at least, hardly one who is a poet in the moral sense of the word) to have waited even this long before expressing his pleasure at this action. We would forgive him this all the more readily because, even in reading, our hearts pause, and gladly detach themselves from the object in order to look within. But of all this, not a trace in Homer; as though he had reported something quite everyday; indeed, as though he possessed no heart in his bosom, he continues in his dry truthfulness:

But Zeus the son of Cronos must have robbed Glaucus of his wits, for he exchanged with Diomedes golden armor for bronze, a hundred oxen's worth for the value of nine.*

Poets of this naive category are no longer at home in an artificial age. They are indeed scarcely even possible, at least in no other wise possible except they *run wild* in their own age, and are preserved by some favorable destiny from its crippling influence. From society itself they can never arise; but from outside it they still sometimes appear, but rather as strangers at

* *Iliad,* Book VI. [Trl. E. V. Rieu, Penguin ed., 1950, p. 123.]

whom one stares, and as uncouth sons of nature by
whom one is irritated. As beneficent as such phenom-
ena are for the artist who studies them and for the
true connoisseur who is able to appreciate them, they
yet elicit little joy on the whole and in their own cen-
tury. The stamp of the conqueror is marked upon their
brows; but we would rather be coddled and indulged
by the Muses. (187) By the critics, the true game-
keepers of taste, they are detested as trespassers whom
one would prefer to suppress; for even Homer owes it
only to the power of more than a thousand years of
testimony that those who sit in judgment on taste per-
mit him to stand; and it is unpleasant enough for them
to maintain their rules against his example and his
reputation against their rules.[15]

[THE SENTIMENTAL POETS (*Die Horen,* No. 12,
1795)]

The poet, I said, either *is* nature or he will *seek* her.
The former is the naive, the latter the sentimental poet.

The poetic spirit is immortal and inalienable in man-
kind, it cannot be lost except together with humanity
or with the capacity for it. For even if man should sep-
arate himself by the freedom of his fantasy and his
understanding from the simplicity, truth and necessity
of nature, yet not only does the way back to her re-
main open always, but also a powerful and ineradica-
ble impulse, the moral, drives him ceaselessly back to
her, and it is precisely with this impulse that the
poetic faculty stands in the most intimate relationship.

Even now, nature is the sole flame at which the
poetic spirit nourishes itself; from her alone it draws

its whole power, to her alone it speaks even in the
artificial man entoiled by civilization. All other modes
of expression are alien to the poetic spirit; hence, gen-
erally speaking, all so-called works of wit are quite
misnamed poetic; although, for long, misled by the
reputation of French literature, we have mistaken
them as such. It is still nature, I say, even now in the
artificial condition of civilization, in virtue of which
the poetic spirit is powerful; but now it stands in quite
another relation to nature.

So long as man is pure—not, of course (188),
crude [16]—nature, he functions as an undivided sensu-
ous unity and as a unifying whole. Sense and reason,
passive and active faculties, are not separated in their
activities, still less do they stand in conflict with one
another. His perceptions are not the formless play of
chance, his thoughts not the empty play of the faculty
of representation; the former proceed out of the law
of *necessity,* the latter out of *actuality.* Once man has
passed into the state of civilization and art has laid
her hand upon him, that *sensuous* harmony in him is
withdrawn, and he can now express himself only as a
moral unity, i.e., as striving after unity. The corre-
spondence between his feeling and thought which in
his first condition *actually* took place, exists now only
ideally; it is no longer within him, but outside of him,
as an idea still to be realized, no longer as a fact in
his life. If one now applies the notion of poetry, which
is nothing but *giving mankind its most complete pos-
sible expression,* to both conditions, the result in the
earlier state of natural simplicity is the completest pos-
sible *imitation of actuality*—at that stage man still
functions with all his powers simultaneously as a har-
monious unity and hence the whole of his nature is

expressed completely in actuality; whereas now, in the state of civilization where that harmonious cooperation of his whole nature is only an idea, it is the elevation of actuality to the ideal or, amounting to the same thing, the *representation of the ideal,* that makes for the poet. And these two are likewise the only possible modes in which poetic genius can express itself at all. They are, as one can see, extremely different from one another, but there is a higher concept under which both can be subsumed, and there should be no surprise if this concept should coincide with the idea of humanity.

(189) This is not the place further to pursue these thoughts, which can only be expounded in full measure in a separate disquisition.[17] But anyone who is capable of making a comparison, based on the spirit and not just on the accidental forms, between ancient and modern poets,* will be able readily to convince himself of the truth of the matter. The former move us by nature, by sensuous truth, by living presence; the latter by ideas.

This path taken by the modern poets is, moreover, that along which man in general, the individual as well as the race, must pass. Nature sets him at one with himself, art divides and cleaves him in two, through the ideal he returns to unity. But because the

* It is perhaps not superfluous to remark that if here the new poets are set over against the ancients, the difference of manner rather than of time is to be understood. We possess in modern times, even most recently, naive works of poetry in all classes, even if no longer of the purest kind and, among the old Latin, even among the Greek poets, there is no lack of sentimental ones. Not only in the same poet, even in the same work one often encounters both species combined, as, for example, in *Werthers Leiden,* and such creations will always produce the greater effects.

ideal is an infinitude to which he never attains, the civilized man can never become perfect in *his* own wise, while the natural man can in his. He must therefore fall infinitely short of the latter in perfection, if one heeds only the relation in which each stands to his species and to his maximum capacity. But if one compares the species with one another, it becomes evident that the goal to which man in civilization *strives* is infinitely preferable to that which he *attains* in nature. For the one obtains its value by the absolute achievement of a finite, (190) the other by approximation to an infinite greatness. But only the latter possesses *degrees* and displays a *progress*, hence the relative worth of a man who is involved in civilization is in general never determinable, even though the same man considered as an individual necessarily finds himself at a disadvantage compared with one in whom nature functions in her utter perfection. But insofar as the ultimate object of mankind is not otherwise to be attained than by that progress, and man cannot progress other than by civilizing himself and hence passing over into the first category, there cannot therefore be any question to which of the two the advantage accrues with reference to that ultimate object.

The very same as has been said of the two different forms of humanity can likewise be applied to those species of poet corresponding to them.

Perhaps on this account one should not compare ancient with modern—naive with sentimental—poets either at all, or only by reference to some higher concept common to both (there is in fact such a concept). For clearly, if one has first abstracted the concept of those species onesidedly from the ancient poets, nothing is easier, but nothing also more trivial, than to depreciate

the moderns by comparison. If one calls poetry only
that which in every age has affected simple nature uni-
formly, the result cannot be other than to deny the
modern poets their title just where they achieve their
most characteristic and sublimest beauty, since pre-
cisely here they speak only to the adherent of civiliza-
tion and have nothing to say to simple nature.* Any-
one whose temperament is not already prepared (191)
to pass beyond actuality into the realm of ideas will
find the richest content empty appearance, and the
loftiest flights of the poet exaggeration. It would not
occur to a reasonable person to want to compare any
modern with Homer where Homer excels, and it
sounds ridiculous enough to find Milton or Klopstock
honored with the title of a modern Homer. But just as
little could any ancient poet, and least of all Homer,
support the comparison with a modern poet in those
aspects which most characteristically distinguish him.
The former, I might put it, is powerful through the art
of finitude; the latter by the art of the infinite.

And for the very reason that the strength of the
ancient artist (for what has been said here of the poet
can, allowing for self-evident qualifications, be ex-

* Molière, as a naive poet, is said to have left it in every case
to the opinion of his chambermaid what should stand or fall in
his comedies; it might also be wished that the masters of the
French buskin had occasionally tried the same experiment with
their tragedies. But I would not advise that a (191) similar
experiment be undertaken with Klopstock's *Odes,* with the
finest passages in the *Messiade,* in *Paradise Lost,* in *Nathan the
Wise,* or in many other pieces. Yet what am I saying?—the
test has really been undertaken, and Molière's chambermaid
chops logic back and forth in our critical literature, philosophi-
cal and belletristic journals and travel accounts, on poetry, art
and the like, as easily, if in poorer taste, on German soil than
on French, as only becomes the servants' hall of German
literature.

tended to apply to the fine arts generally) subsists in
finitude, the great advantage arises which the plastic
art of antiquity maintains over that of modern times,
and in general the unequal value relationship in which
the modern art of poetry and modern plastic art stand
to both species of art in antiquity. A work addressed
to the eye can achieve perfection only in finitude; a
work addressed to the imagination can achieve it also
through the infinite. In plastic art works the modern is
little aided by his superiority in ideas; here (192) he
is obliged to *determine in space in the most precise
way* the representation of his imagination and hence
to compete with the ancient artists in precisely that
quality in which they indisputably excel. In poetic
works it is otherwise, and even if the ancient poets are
victorious too in the simplicity of forms and in what-
ever is sensuously representable and *corporeal,* the
modern can nonetheless leave them behind in richness
of material in whatever is insusceptible of representa-
tion and ineffable, in a word, in whatever in the work
of art is called *spirit.*

Since the naive poet only follows simple nature and
feeling, and limits himself solely to imitation of actu-
ality, he can have only a single relationship to his sub-
ject and in *this* respect there is for him no choice in
his treatment. The varied impression of naive poetry
depends (provided that one puts out of mind every-
thing which in it belongs to the content, and consid-
ers that impression only as the pure product of the
poetic treatment) it depends, I say, solely upon the
various degrees of one and the same mode of feeling;
even the variety of external forms cannot effect any
alteration in the quality of that aesthetic impression.
The form may be lyric or epic, dramatic or narrative:

we can indeed be moved to a weaker or stronger degree, but (as soon as the matter is abstracted) never heterogeneously. Our feeling is uniformly the same, entirely composed of *one* element, so that we cannot differentiate within it. Even the difference of language and era changes nothing in this regard, for just this pure unity of its origin and of its effect is a characteristic of naive poetry.

The case is quite otherwise with the sentimental poet. He *reflects* upon the impression that objects make upon him, and only in that reflection is the emotion grounded which he himself experiences and which he excites in us. The object here (193) is referred to an idea and his poetic power is based solely upon this referral. The sentimental poet is thus always involved with two conflicting representations and perceptions— with actuality as a limit and with his idea as infinitude; and the mixed feelings that he excites will always testify to this dual source.* Since in this case there is a plurality of principles it depends which of the two will *predominate* in the perception of the poet and in his representation, and hence a variation in the treatment is possible. For now the question arises whether he will tend more toward actuality or toward the ideal

---

* Anyone who observes the impression that naive poetry makes on him and is able to separate from it that part which is due to the content will find this impression always joyous, always pure, always serene, even in the case of very pathetic objects; with sentimental poetry it will always be somewhat solemn and intense. This is because with naive accounts, regardless of their subject matter, we always rejoice in our imagination in the truth, in the living presence of the object, and seek nothing further beyond these; whereas with the sentimental we have to reconcile the representation of imagination with an idea of reason and hence always fluctuate between two different conditions.

—whether he will realize the former as an object of antipathy or the latter as an object of sympathy. His presentation will, therefore, be either *satirical* or it will be (in a broader connotation of the word which will become clearer later) *elegiac;* every sentimental poet will adhere to one of these two modes of perception.

[*Satirical Poetry*]

The poet is satirical if he takes as his subject alienation from nature and the contradiction between actuality and the ideal (in their effect upon the mind both amount to the same thing). (194) But this he can execute either seriously and with passion, or jokingly and with good humor, according as he dwells in the realm of will or the realm of understanding. The former is a function of punitive or pathetic satire, the latter of playful satire.

Strictly speaking, the poet's purpose is compatible neither with the accent of correction nor with that of amusement. The former is too solemn for that play which poetry should always be; the latter too frivolous for the solemnity which must underlie all poetic play.[18] Moral contradictions necessarily interest our hearts and therefore deprive our minds of their freedom; yet every substantive interest, i.e., any reference to a necessity, should be banished from poetic emotion. Contradictions of the understanding, on the other hand, leave the heart indifferent, and yet the poet is concerned with the highest promptings of the heart, with nature, and with the ideal. Hence it is no small task for him in pathetic satire to avoid doing injury to the poetic form which subsists in freedom of play; and in playful satire not to fall short of the poetic content which must always be the infinite. This undertaking can be resolved only in a single manner. Punitive satire achieves poetic freedom by passing over into the sublime; playful satire obtains poetic content by treating its subject with beauty.

In satire, actuality is contrasted with the highest reality as falling short of the ideal. It is, moreover, quite unnecessary that this be articulated, provided only that the poet is able to intimate this to the mind; but this he absolutely must do or it will not function poetically at all. Actuality is here therefore a necessary object of antipathy; but—and this is all-important— this antipathy must itself necessarily arise out of the opposed ideal. For it could in fact have a sensuous origin and be grounded merely in *some inner need* (195) with which actuality is in conflict; and often enough we feel moral indignation at the world, when it is only the conflict between the world and our inclination that embitters us.[19] It is this material interest that the vulgar satirist exploits, and since he can hardly fail by this method to arouse our emotion, he believes he has conquered our hearts, and that he is a master of pathos. But any pathos deriving from this source is unworthy of the art of poetry, which may touch us only through ideas and approach our hearts only by the path of reason. In addition, this impure and material pathos will always reveal itself by an excess of passion and through a painful embarrassment of the intellect, whereas truly poetic pathos can be recognized by a predominance of spontaneity and by a freedom of spirit which still survives even in emotion. For if the emotion arises out of the ideal that confronts actuality, then all inhibiting feelings are lost in the sublimity of the former, and the greatness of the idea with which we are filled elevates us above all the limitations of experience. In the representation of offending actuality everything depends therefore upon necessity's being the basis on which the poet or narrator presents the actual, if he is to be able to attune our spirits to ideas. If only *we* remain lofty in our judgment nothing is lost if the subject remains base and far beneath us. When the historian Tacitus depicts for us the profound depravity of the Romans of the first century he is still a superior spirit who looks down upon the base, and our mood is truly poetic because only the height where he himself stands and to which he was able to elevate us makes his subject base.

Pathetic satire must, therefore, always derive from a temperament that is vigorously permeated by the ideal. Only a predominant impulse toward harmony (196) can and may produce that profound sense of moral contradiction and that burning indignation against moral perversity which becomes the inspiration of a Juvenal, a Swift, a Rousseau, a Haller,[20] and others. These poets would and must have written with the same felicity also in the more moving and tender forms if fortuitous causes had not given this definite tendency to their temperaments; and this they have actually done to some extent. All those mentioned have lived either in a depraved era and saw before them a fearful spectacle of moral decay, or their own fates had sown bitterness in their souls. Even the philosophical spirit, since he separates with implacable rigor appearances from essence, and penetrates into the depths of things, inclines to that severity and austerity with which Rousseau, Haller, and others depict actuality. But these extraneous and coincidental influences which always have an inhibiting effect may at most determine the tendency only, never supply the content of inspiration. This must be the same in everyone and, free of every external constraint, must flow out of a burning impulse for the ideal which is absolutely the only true vocation for the satiric as for the sentimental poet in general.

If pathetic satire is appropriate only to sublime souls, playful satire will succeed only with a beautiful soul. For the first is already secured from frivolity by its serious subject; but the second, which may treat only a morally neutral subject, would lapse unavoidably into frivolity, and lose all poetic value if in this case the manner did not ennoble the matter and the poet's *personality* did not stand in place of his *theme*. But it is given only to the beautiful heart in all its utterances to impress a complete image of itself independently of the subject of its activity. The sublime character can manifest itself only in discrete victories over the resistance of the (197) senses, only in certain instants of impetus and momentary effort; but in the beautiful soul the ideal functions as nature, that is, uniformly, and hence can reveal itself even in a state of calm. The fathomless sea appears most sublime in its motion, the pellucid brook most beautiful in its serene flow.

It has frequently been disputed which of the two, tragedy or comedy, merits precedence over the other. If the question is merely which of the two treats of the more important subject matter, there can be no doubt that the first has the advantage; but if one would know which of the two demands the more significant poet, then the decision may rather fall to the latter. In tragedy much is already determined by the substance, in comedy nothing is determined by the substance and everything by the poet. Since in judg-

ments of taste the content is never taken into account
it follows naturally that the aesthetic value of these
two artistic genres stands in inverse proportion to their
substantive significance. The tragic poet is supported
by his theme, the comic poet on the other hand must
raise his to aesthetic height through his own person.
The first may make a leap for which, however, not
much is required; the other must remain himself, he
must therefore already *be* there and be at home there
where the first cannot attain without a starting leap.
And it is precisely in this way that the beautiful char-
acter is distinguished from the sublime. In the first, all
the dimensions are already contained, flowing uncon-
strainedly and effortlessly by its nature and it is, ac
cording to its capacity, an infinitude at every point in
its path; the other can elevate and exert itself to any
dimension, by the power of its will it can tear itself
out of any state of limitation. The latter is, then, only
intermittently and with effort free, the former with
facility and always.

To promote and nourish this freedom of tempera-
ment (198) is the fair task of comedy just as tragedy
is destined to help to restore by aesthetic means the
freedom of temperament when it has been violently
disrupted by emotion. In tragedy, therefore, freedom
of temperament must be artificially and experimentally
disrupted, since it displays its poetic power in the res-
toration of that freedom; in comedy, on the other
hand, care must be taken to assure that that disruption
of the freedom of temperament should never occur.
Hence the tragic poet always treats his subject prac-
tically, the comic poet always treats his theoretically,
even if the former should indulge the quirk (like Les-
sing in his *Nathan*) of treating a theoretical subject, or

of the latter of treating a practical subject. Not the
sphere from which the subject is drawn, but the forum
before which the poet brings it makes it tragic or
comic. The tragedian must beware of calm reasoning
and always engage the heart; the comedian must be-
ware of pathos and always entertain the understand-
ing. The former thus displays his art by the constant
excitement of passion, the latter by constant avoid-
ance of it; and this art is naturally so much the greater
on both parts the more the subject of one is of an
abstract nature, and that of the other tends toward the
pathetic.* Even if tragedy proceeds from a more sig-
nificant point, one is obliged to concede, on the other
hand, that comedy proceeds toward a more significant
purpose and it would, were it to attain it, render all
tragedy superfluous and impossible. Its purpose is uni-
form with the highest after which man has to struggle,
to be free of passion, (199) always clear, to look
serenely about and within himself, to find everywhere
more coincidence than fate, and rather to laugh at
absurdity than to rage or weep at malice.

As in actual life, it often happens in poetic works
also that mere frivolity, pleasing talent, amiable good

* In *Nathan the Wise* this is not the case; here the frosty na-
ture of the theme has cooled the whole art work. But Lessing
himself knew that he was not writing a tragedy and simply for-
got in his own case, humanly enough, his own doctrine pro-
pounded in the *Dramaturgy* that the poet is not permitted to
employ the tragic form for other than a tragic purpose. With-
out very substantial (199) changes it would hardly be possible
to transform this dramatic poem into a good tragedy; but with
merely incidental changes it might have yielded a good
comedy. For the latter purpose the pathetic would have to be
sacrificed, for the former its reasoning, and there can be no
question upon which of the two the beauty of the poem most
depends. [Translator's note: cf. the posthumous fragment (XII
330, 18 ff.) on this issue.]

humor, are confused for beauty of soul, and since the vulgar taste can never raise itself above the pleasant it is easy enough for such *lightsome* spirits to usurp the fame which is so difficult to earn. But there is an infallible test by means of which lightness of disposition can be distinguished from lightness of the ideal, as well as virtue of temperament from true morality of character, and this is when both confront a difficult and great theme. In such a case the precious genius inevitably collapses into the banal, as does virtue of temperament [21] into the material; the truly beautiful soul, however, passes over as certainly into the sublime.

So long as Lucian [22] merely castigates absurdity, as in the *Wishes*, the *Lapithae*, in *Zeus Rants*, etc., he remains a mocker and delights us with his joyful humor; but he becomes quite another man in many passages of his *Nigrinus*, his *Timon*, his *Alexander*, in which his satire strikes also at moral decay. "Unhappy wretch," he begins in his *Nigrinus* the shocking picture of contemporary Rome, "why did you leave the light of the sun, (200) Greece, and that happy life of freedom, and come here into this turmoil of sumptuous servitude, of dancing attendance, of banquets, of sycophants, flatterers, poisoners, legacy-hunters, and false friends?" etc. On this and similar occasions is revealed the high solemnity of feeling that must underlie all play if it is to be poetic. Even in the malicious joke with which Lucian as well as Aristophanes abuses Socrates one perceives a serious reason which avenges truth upon the sophist—battles on behalf of an ideal that it does not always articulate. The first of these two, in his *Diogenes* and *Demonax*, has justified this character beyond all doubt; among moderns, what a

great and noble character has Cervantes expressed on
every worthy occasion in his *Don Quixote*! What a
magnificent ideal must have dwelt in the soul of the
poet who created a Tom Jones and a Sophia! How
readily can laughing Yorick [23] touch our minds at will
so loftily and so powerfully! In our own Wieland also
I recognize this seriousness of feeling; even the wan-
ton play of his moods is ensouled and ennobled by
grace of heart; even in the rhythm of his song its im-
press is manifest, and he never lacks the impetus to
carry us, if the moment is apt, to the greatest heights.

No comparable judgment can be passed on Vol-
taire's satire. True enough, even with this writer it is
still only the truth and simplicity of nature by which
he sometimes moves us poetically, either because he
really attains to it in a naive character, as frequently in
his *Ingénu*, or because he seeks and defends it, as in
Candide, etc. If neither of these two is the case then
he may indeed amuse us as a witty fellow, but cer-
tainly not as a poet. Everywhere too little seriousness
underlies his ridicule, and this justly brings his poetic
vocation under suspicion. (201) We perpetually en-
counter only his understanding, never his feeling. No
ideal is manifest beneath that airy frame and scarcely
anything absolutely fixed in that ceaseless motion. Far
from displaying any evidence for the inner abundance
of his spirit, his wonderful variety of external forms
gives rather a dubious testimony to the opposite effect,
for despite all those forms he has not found even *one*
upon which to leave the impress of his heart. One
must therefore almost fear that in this richly endowed
genius it was only poverty of feeling that determined
his satiric vocation. Had this been otherwise he must
surely somewhere along his broad career have de-

parted from this narrow way. But despite the tremendous variety of content and external form we see the endless recurrence of this inner form in all its indigent uniformity, and despite his massive career he never fulfilled in himself the cycle of humanity which one joyfully finds permeating the satirists mentioned above.

[Elegiac Poetry]

If the poet should set nature and art, the ideal and actuality, in such opposition that the representation of the first prevails and pleasure in it becomes the predominant feeling, then I call him *elegiac*. This category, too, like satire, comprehends two species. Either nature and the ideal are an object of sadness if the first is treated as lost and the second as unattained. Or both are an object of joy represented as actual. The first yields the *elegy* in the narrower sense, and the second the idyll in the broader sense.*

---

* That I employ the terms satire, elegy, and idyll in a wider sense than is customary, I will hardly have to explain to readers who penetrate deeper into the matter. My intention in doing so is by no means to disrupt the boundaries which have been set for good reasons by usage hitherto for satire and elegy as well as idyll; I look merely at the *mode of perception* predominant in these poetic categories, and it (202) is sufficiently well known that these cannot be accommodated at all within those narrow limits. We are not moved elegiacally solely by the elegy which is exclusively so called: the dramatic and epic poets can also move us in the elegiac manner. In the *Messiah*, in Thomson's *Seasons*, in *Paradise Lost*, in *Jerusalem Delivered*, we find numerous depictions which are otherwise proper only to the idyll, the elegy, and to satire. Likewise, to a greater or lesser degree, in almost every pathetic poem. But that I account the idyll itself as an elegiac category does seem to require justification. It should be recalled, though, that here I speak only of that kind of idyll that is a species of sentimental

Just as indignation from the pathetic, and mockery from the playful, satire, sadness may derive from elegy (203) only from enthusiasm awakened by the ideal. Only thus does elegy receive poetic content, and every other source of it is beneath the dignity of the art of poetry. The elegiac poet seeks nature, but in her beauty, not merely in her pleasantness, in her correspondence with ideas, not just in her acquiescence in necessity. Sadness at lost joys, at the golden age now disappeared from the world, at happiness departed with youth, with love, and so forth, can only become the material of an elegiac poem if those states of sensuous satisfaction can also be construed as matters of

---

poetry, to the essence of which belongs the notion that nature is *opposed* to art, and the ideal to actuality. Even if this is not rendered explicit by the artist and he offers to our view a pure and spontaneous portrait of unspoiled nature or of the ideal fulfilled, yet that opposition is still within his heart and will betray itself in every stroke of the brush, even against his will. For even if this were not so, then the very language which he must employ, because it bears the spirit of the age and has undergone the influence of art, would serve to remind us of actuality and its limitations, of civilization with its mannerism; indeed, our own heart would oppose to that picture of pure nature its experience of corruption and thus render the mode of perception elegiac in us even though this had not been sought by the poet. This last is so unavoidable that even the highest delight which the finest works of the naive genus of ancient and modern times assure to the cultivated individual do not for long remain pure, but sooner or later will be accompanied by an elegiac mood. Finally, I would still observe that the division attempted here, for the very reason that it is simply based on the distinction of mode of perception, should by no means whatever determine the division of poetry itself nor the derivation of poetic genres; since the poet is in no way bound, even in a single work, to the same mode of perception, that division therefore cannot apply, (203) but must be taken from the form of the presentation.

moral harmony. Thus I cannot consider the lamenta-
tions of Ovid which he chanted from his place of exile
on the Black Sea, moving as they are and containing
so much that is poetic in individual passages, as being
as a whole a poetic work. There is far too little energy,
far too little spirit and nobility in his pain. Necessity,
not inspiration, utters those laments; in them breathes,
if not actually a vulgar soul, yet the vulgar mood of a
finer spirit that has been crushed by its fate. Still,
when we recall that it is Rome and the Rome of Au-
gustus for which he sorrows, we forgive the son of
pleasure his pain; but even magnificent Rome, with
all its enchantments, is still (if the power of imagina-
tion has not first ennobled it) only a finite quantity,
hence an unworthy object for the poetic art which,
superior to everything that actuality has to offer, pos-
sesses the right to mourn only for the infinite.

The content of poetic lamentation can therefore
never be an external object, it must always be only an
ideal, inner one; even if it grieves over some loss in
actuality, it must first be transformed into an ideal
(204) loss. In this assimilation of the finite to the in-
finite, poetic treatment in fact subsists. The external
matter is, therefore, always indifferent in itself since
the poetic art can never employ it as it occurs, but
only by means of what poetry makes of it does it
receive its poetic value. The elegiac poet seeks nature,
but as an idea and in a perfection in which she has
never existed, when he bemourns her at once as some-
thing having existed and now lost. When Ossian tells
of the days which are no more, and of the heroes who
have disappeared, his poetic power has long since
transformed those images of recollection into ideals,
and those heroes into gods. The experience of a par-

ticular loss has been broadened into the idea of universal evanescence and the bard, affected and pursued by the image of omnipresent ruin, elevates himself to the skies to find there, in the cycle of the sun, an image of the immutable.*

I turn now to the modern poets of the elegiac category. Rousseau, both as poet and as philosopher, reveals no other tendency but either to seek nature or to vindicate her by art. According as his feeling dwells on one or the other we find him sometimes elegiacally moved, sometimes, as in his *Julie,* enraptured in the realm of the idyll. Unquestionably his poems possess poetic content, since they are concerned with an ideal; but he does not know how to exploit it in a poetic manner. His serious character never permits him, it is true, to sink to frivolity, but it does not permit him either to rise to poetic play. Sometimes, gripped by passion, sometimes by abstraction, he rarely or never achieves the aesthetic freedom which the poet must maintain in relation to his material and communicate to his listener. Either it is his unhealthy (205) excess of feeling which overpowers him and renders his emotion painful; or it is his excess of thought that lays shackles upon his imagination, and by the rigor of his concepts destroys the grace of the depiction. Both characteristics, whose inner reciprocal workings and reconciliation in fact make for the poet, are present in this writer to an unusually high degree, and nothing is lacking except that they should manifest themselves in actual unison, that his intellectual activity should be combined with his feeling, and his sensitivity more combined with his thought. Hence, in the ideal that he

---

* See, for example, the superb poem entitled *Carthon.*

established for humanity, too much emphasis is laid upon man's limitations and too little upon his capacities; and in it one observes everywhere a need for physical calm rather than for moral harmony. His passionate sensitivity is to blame for preferring to restore man to the spiritless uniformity of his first state in order simply to be rid of the conflict within him, rather than to look for the termination of that conflict in the spiritual harmony of a completely fulfilled education; he would rather that art had never begun than that he should await its consummation; in a word, he would rather set his aim lower and degrade his ideal only in order to attain to it the more quickly and more surely.

Among German poets of this order I will mention here only Haller, Kleist,[24] and Klopstock. The character of their poetry is sentimental; they touch us by ideas, not by sensuous truth; not so much because they are nature as because they are able to inspire enthusiasm in us for nature. Whatever, therefore, is true of the character of these as well as of all sentimental poets *in general* naturally does not by any means exclude the capacity *in particular* to move us by naive beauty; without this they would not be poets at all. But it is not their essential and predominant character to feel with serene, simple, and unencumbered senses and to present again what they have felt (206) in like manner. Involuntarily imagination crowds out sense and thought feeling, and they close their eyes and ears to sink into internal reflection. The mind cannot tolerate any impression without at once observing its own activity and reflection, and yielding up in terms of itself whatever it has absorbed. In this mode we are never given the subject, only what the reflective understanding has made of it, and even when the poet is

himself the subject, if he would describe his feeling to
us, we never learn of his condition directly and at first
hand, but rather how he has reflected in his own mind,
what he has thought about it as an observer of himself.
When Haller is lamenting the death of his wife (in a
well known poem), and begins as follows:

> Shall I sing of thy death?
> O Mariane, what a song!
> When sighs contest with words
> And one idea flees before the rest, etc.

then we may indeed find this description exactly true,
but we feel also that the poet has not actually com-
municated his feelings but his thought about the mat-
ter. He therefore moves us much more feebly also, be-
cause he must himself have been very much cooler to
be an observer of his own emotion.

The predominantly supersensuous material alone of
Haller's and, in part, of Klopstock's poetry excludes
them from the naive category; hence, for that material
to be poetically treated, it must (since it cannot as-
sume any corporeal nature and in consequence cannot
become an object of sensuous intuition) be translated
into the eternal and be elevated into an object of spir-
itual intuition. Generally speaking, didactic poetry
can only be conceived of without inner contradiction
in this sense; for, to repeat this once again, the art of
poetry comprehends these two realms only: (207)
either it must dwell in the world of sense or in the
world of ideas, since it absolutely cannot flourish in
the realm of concepts or in the world of understand-
ing. I confess that I have yet to encounter the poem of
this order either in ancient or modern literature that
was able to lead the concept which it treated purely

and completely either downward to individuality or upward to the idea. It is usually the case, when it is successful at all, that the poem fluctuates between both, while the abstract concept dominates, and imagination, which should be in command in the poetic realm, is simply subordinated to the service of the understanding. The didactic poem in which the thought is itself poetic and remains so has yet to be seen.

What has been said here in general about all didactic poetry applies in particular to Haller. The thought itself is not poetic, but the execution sometimes is, either by the employment of the images, or by its soaring to ideas. Only in this latter quality do they belong here. Strength and profundity and a pathetic seriousness characterize this poet. His spirit is kindled by an ideal and his glowing feeling for truth seeks in the stilly alpine valleys the innocence that has disappeared from the world. His lament is deeply moving: with energetic, almost bitter satire, he marks the distractions of understanding and heart; and with love the beautiful simplicity of nature. But the concept predominates everywhere in his descriptions, just as within himself understanding dominates over feeling. Hence, he *teaches* throughout more than he *represents,* and represents throughout more with powerful than with attractive strokes. He is great, daring, fiery, sublime; but he rarely, if ever, raises his work to beauty.

Kleist is far inferior to him in the content of his ideas and depth of spirit; in grace (208) he may be superior to him if we do not, as sometimes happens, account his weakness in the one aspect as a strength in the other. Kleist's emotion-laden soul expands most at the spectacle of rural scenes and usages. Gladly he escapes

from the empty turmoil of society and finds in the
bosom of inanimate nature the harmony and peace
that he misses in the moral world. How affecting is his
longing for calm! * How true and how felt when he
sings:

> Aye, world, thou truly art the grave of life.
> Often am I urged by an impulse to virtue,
> And melancholy draws many a tear down my cheek,
> Example is victorious, and thou, oh fire of youth:
> Together drying up those noble tears.

To be true to humanity one must be far from men.
Yet, if his poetic impulse has led him away from the
constricting round of circumstances into the spiritual
loneliness of nature, still he is pursued even this far by
the anxious image of the age and unfortunately, too, by
its fetters. What he flees lies within him, what he
seeks is forever outside him; he can never overcome
the bale influence of his generation. Even if his heart
is sufficiently afire, his fantasy energetic enough, to
ensoul the dead configurations of his understanding
by his composition, still cold thought as often deprives
the living creation of his poetic powers of its soul, and
reflection disrupts the secret labor of feeling. His
poetry is indeed as bright and sparkling as the spring
that he celebrates in song, his fantasy is live and ac-
tive; yet one must call it evanescent rather than rich,
playful rather than creative, uneasily progressing
rather than unifying and plastic. Rapidly and luxuri-
antly its features change, but without crystallizing
themselves into a whole, without becoming filled with
life and rounding themselves into a unity. So long as
he merely writes lyrically and merely dwells upon

* See the poem of this name in his works.

landscape images, partly the greater freedom (209) of
lyrical form, partly the more arbitrary quality of his
material permits us to overlook this shortcoming, since
in this case we always demand the representation of
the poet's feelings rather than of the subject itself. But
the mistake becomes only too obvious when he goes
out of his way, as in his *Cissides and Paches* and his
Seneca, to depict human beings and human actions;
for here the imaginative power finds itself hemmed in
amid fixed and necessary limits, and the poetic effect
can proceed only from the *subject.* Here he becomes
insipid, dull, thin, and all but insupportably cold: an
admonition to anyone who tries without inner vocation
to project himself from the field of musical into the
realm of plastic poetry. A similiar genius, Thomson,
fell victim to the same, only human, feeling.[25]

In the sentimental genus, and particularly in the
elegiac species of it, few poets of modern times and
fewer still of antiquity may be compared with our
Klopstock. Whatever could be attained in the realm of
ideality, outside the boundaries of living form and out-
side the sphere of individuality, has been achieved by
this musical poet.* One would indeed do him a grave
injustice (210) if one were altogether to deny him that
individual truth and vivacity with which the naive

* I say *musical* to recall here the dual relationship of poetry
with music and plastic art. According as poetry either imitates
a given *object* as the plastic arts do, or whether, like music,
simply produces a given *state of mind,* without requiring a
given object for the purpose, it can be called plastic or musical.
The latter expression, therefore, does not refer exclusively to
whatever is music in poetry actually and in relation to its ma-
terial, but rather in general to all those effects which it is able
to produce without subordinating the imagination to a given
object; and in this sense I call Klopstock a musical poet above
all.

poet depicts his theme. Many of his odes, several individual features of his dramas and of his *Messiah* portray the object with striking veracity and with beautiful circumscription; particularly where the object is his own heart, he has not infrequently displayed a lofty nature, an enchanting naivety. But *his* strength does not lie in this, this characteristics is not to be fulfilled throughout the whole of his poetic range. As superb a creation as the *Messiah* is in the *musical* poetic sense as defined above, yet much is left to be desired from the *plastic* poetic point of view in which one expects specific forms and forms *specific for sensuous intuition*. The personages in this poem may perhaps be specific enough, but not for intuition; abstraction alone has created them, only abstraction can distinguish them. They are fine examples of concepts, but not individuals, not living figures. It is left much too much to the imagination, to which nonetheless the poet must return and which he should command by the thoroughgoing specificity of his forms, in what manner these men and angels, this God and Satan, this heaven and this hell shall embody themselves. An outline is given within which the understanding must necessarily conceive of them, but no firm boundary is set within which fantasy must necessarily portray them. What I say here of the characters applies to everything that is or should be life and action in this poem; and not just in the epic, but also in the dramatic works of our poet. For the understanding everything is finely delineated and delimited (I mention here only his Judas, his Pilate, his Philo, his Salomo in the tragedy of that name), but it is far too formless for the imagination and here, I freely confess, I find the poet entirely out of his sphere.

(211) His sphere is always the realm of ideas, and he is able to transport everything he touches into the infinite. One might say he witnesses the matter out of everything he touches so as to transform it into spirit, just as other poets endow everything spiritual with matter. Virtually every pleasure that his poetry affords must be gained by the exercise of thought; all the feelings, however fervent and powerful, that he is able to engender in us stream forth from supersensuous sources. Hence the seriousness, the power, the impetus, the depth that characterizes everything that comes from him; hence also the perennial tension of the mind in which we are maintained in reading him. No poet (with the possible exception of Young,[25a] who demands more in this respect than Klopstock but without compensating for it as he does) would seem to be less apt to become a favorite and companion through life than Klopstock, who always leads us only away from life, always summons up only the spirit, without vivifying the senses with the serene presence of an object. His poetical muse is chaste, supermundane, incorporeal, holy, like his religion, and one must confess with admiration that even though he may sometimes go astray on these heights, he still has never fallen from them. I admit, therefore, without reserve, that I am somewhat fearful for the temperament of anyone who really and without affectation can make this poet his favorite reading, the kind of reading to which one can attune oneself in any mood, to which one can return from any mood; also, it would seem to me, we have seen enough in Germany of the fruits of his dangerous domination. Only in certain exalted frames of mind can he be sought out and appreciated; for this reason, too, he is the idol of the young, if by far not

their happiest choice. Youth, which always strives beyond the conditions of life, which escapes from all forms and finds any limitation too constricting, abandons itself with love and delight in the endless expanses opened up to it by this poet. (212) But when the boy becomes a man and returns from the realm of ideas into the limitations of experience, then much is lost, very much of that enthusiastic love, but not of the respect which is due to so unique a phenomenon, to so extraordinary a genius, to such very ennobled feeling, a respect which the German owes to such high merit.[26]

I called this poet great above all in the elegiac species, and it will hardly be necessary to justify this judgment in further detail. Equal to every effort and master of the entire range of sentimental poetry, he can now shake us with the highest pathos, now soothe us with celestially tender feelings; but above all his heart is inclined to a lofty spirit-filled melancholy and, as sublime as his harp, his lyre sounds, yet the melting tones of his lute [26a] will still ring truer and more deeply and movingly. I appeal to every purely attuned feeling and ask whether it would not gladly abandon everything bold and powerful, every fiction, every superb description, every model of oratorical eloquence in the *Messiah*, all the glittering similes in which our poet is so outstandingly successful—whether it would abandon all this for the sake of the tender feelings that are breathed forth in the elegy *To Ebert*, in the splendid poems *Bardale, Early Graves, Summer Night, Lake Zurich*, and many of this order. For as dear to me as the *Messiah* is as a treasure of elegiac feelings and ideal portrayals, it satisfies me less as the depiction of action or as an epic work.

Perhaps, before leaving this field, I should refer also to the merits of Uz, Denis, Gessner (in his *Death of Abel*), Jacobi, von Gerstenberg, of Hölty, von Göckingk,[27] and many others of this class, who all move us through ideas and, in the sense of the word defined above, have written as sentimental poets. But my purpose is not (213) to write a history of German poetry, but to illustrate what has been said by a few examples out of our literature. It was the variety of the path that I wanted to show, by which ancient and modern, naive and sentimental poets proceed to the same goal —that if the former move us through nature, individuality, and living *sensuousness*, the latter, by ideas and lofty *spirituality*, manifest an equally great, if not so widespread, power over our minds.

From the previous examples it could be seen how the sentimental poetic spirit treats a natural theme; but one might also be interested in knowing how the naive poetic spirit proceeds with a sentimental theme. This task appears to be completely new and of a quite unique difficulty, for in the ancient and naive world a *theme* of this kind did not occur, whereas in the modern the *poet* would be lacking. Nevertheless, genius has accepted this task also and has resolved it in an admirably felicitous manner. A personality who embraces the ideal with burning feeling and abandons actuality in order to contend with an insubstantial infinitude, who seeks continuously outside himself for that which he continuously destroys within himself, to whom only his dreams are the real, his experience perennial limitations, who in the end sees in his own existence only a limitation, and, as is reasonable, tears this down in order to penetrate to the true reality— this dangerous extreme of the sentimental personality has become the theme of a poet in whom nature functions more faithfully and purely than any other, and who, among modern poets, is perhaps least removed from the sensuous truth of things.

It is interesting to note with what fortunate instinct everything that nourishes the sentimental character is concentrated in *Werther*: fanatically unhappy love, sensitivity (214) to nature, feeling for religion, a spirit of philosophical contemplation; finally, so that nothing shall be forgotten, the gloomy, formless, melancholic Ossianic world. If one takes account with how little recommendation, even in how hostile a manner actuality is contrasted with it, and how everything external unites to drive the tortured youth back into his world of ideals, then one sees no possibility how such a character could have saved himself from such a cycle. In the same poet's *Tasso* the same opposition occurs, albeit in quite different characters; even in his latest novel,[28] just as in that first one, the poetic spirit is set in opposition to plain common sense, the ideal over against the actual, the subjective mode of representation over against the objective—but with what a difference!; even in *Faust* we encounter the same opposition, of course insofar as the theme requires it, very coarsened and materialized on both sides; [29] it is well worth the effort to attempt to analyze the psychological development of this personality as it is manifested in four such different ways.

It was observed earlier that the merely carefree and jovial type of mind, when it is not based on an inner wealth of ideas, fails to yield a vocation for playful satire, as readily as popular opinion would assume this; just as little does merely tender effeminacy and melancholy provide a vocation for elegiac poetry.

Both are lacking that principle of energy that belongs to the true poetic gift, and that must animate its subject matter in order to produce the truly beautiful. Products of this delicate sort can, therefore, only melt us and, without enlivening the heart and engaging the spirit, they merely flatter sensuousness. A continuous tendency to this mode of feeling must, at the last, necessarily enervate the character and depress it into a condition of passivity out of which no reality at all can proceed, either for the external nor the inner life. It was, therefore, altogether warranted to pursue with implacable mockery that evil of *affected* (215) *feeling** and *lachrymose demeanor* which, as a result of the misunderstanding and aping of a few excellent works, began to gain the upper hand in Germany about 18 years ago,[30] even though the indulgence which there is a tendency to display toward the scarcely better counterpart of that elegiac caricature, toward facetious manners, toward heartless satire and pointless caprices * makes it clear enough that they are not being exclaimed against for entirely pure rea-

* "The tendency," as Herr Adelung defines it, "to sensitive, tender feelings without a rational intention and beyond due measure."—Herr Adelung is very fortunate that he feels only by intention, and even only by rational intention.
* The wretched pleasures of certain readers should not, indeed, be marred, and in the final analysis, what concern is it of criticism if there are people who can regale and edify themselves with the sordid wit of Herr Blumauer. But the judges of art should at least refrain from speaking with a certain respect of works the existence of which might decently remain a secret from good taste. One cannot, indeed, mistake either the talent or the caprice they contain, but it is all the more to be regretted that both qualities are not more purified. I say nothing of our German comedies; the poets depict the age in which they live. [Translator's note: Alois Blumauer (1755-98), a low-grade Austrian humorist.]

sons. In the scales of genuine taste the one must have as little effect as the other, for both lack the aesthetic content which is contained only in the inmost combination of spirit and matter, and in the unified relation of a work to the faculties of feeling and ideas.

Siegwart and his cloister story have been mocked, and the *Journey to Southern France* [31] is admired; yet both works have an equal claim to a certain degree of appreciation; and an equally small one to unqualified praise. True, if extravagant, feeling makes for the value of the first novel, a delicate humor and a vivaciously (216) fine understanding for the second; but just as the first is entirely lacking in appropriate sobriety of understanding, the second is lacking in aesthetic dignity. The first is a little ridiculous in the light of experience, the other virtually contemptible compared with the ideal. But since the truly beautiful must correspond on the one hand with nature and on the other with the ideal, the first can lay as little claim as the second to the name of a beautiful work. Nonetheless it is natural and reasonable and I know from my own experience that Thümmel's novel is read with great pleasure. Since he offends only against those demands that originate in the ideal, which in consequence are not imposed at all by the greatest number of his readers and never by the better ones if they are reading a novel, yet he fulfills in no mean degree the remaining demands of the spirit—and of the body —and hence his must and will justifiably remain a favored book of our and every age in which aesthetic works are written simply in order to please, and are read simply for pleasure.

But does not poetic literature possess even classical works which offend the lofty purity of the ideal in a like manner, and which seem by the materiality of their content to be very far removed from that spirituality which we here demand of every aesthetic work of art? What even the poet, that chaste apostle of the muse, may permit himself, should that be denied to the novelist, who is only his half-brother and still so very much earthbound? I can all the less avoid this question here since there exist in the elegiac as well as in the satiric class masterpieces in which a quite other nature from that of which this essay treats is sought, recommended, and gives the appearance of being defended not only against evil morals but also against good morals. Hence, either these poetic works would have to be rejected (217), or the concept established here of elegiac poetry must be taken as much too abitrary.

Whatever the poet may permit himself, was the question; should that be withheld from the prose narrator? The answer is already contained in the question: whatever is permitted the poet can prove nothing for one who is not a poet. In the concept itself of poet, and only in this, lies the ground of that freedom which is merely contemptible license as soon as it is not derived from the highest and noblest that constitutes him.

The laws of propriety are alien to innocent nature; only the experience of corruption has given them their origin. But as soon as that experience has been undergone and natural innocence has disappeared from morals, then they become sacred laws which a moral feeling may not contravene. They apply in any artificial world with the same right as the laws of nature rule in the world of innocence. But it is precisely this that denotes the poet: that he revokes everything in

himself that recalls an artificial world, that he is able
to restore nature within himself to her original sim-
plicity. But having done this, then he is by the same
token exempted from all laws by which a corrupted
heart is protected against itself. He is pure, he is in-
nocent, and whatever is permitted to innocent nature
is permitted him too; if you, who read or listen to
him, are no longer guiltless, and if you cannot become
so for the moment through his purifying presence,
then it is *your* misfortune, not his; you are forsaking
him, he has not sung for you.

The following, then, may be said with reference to
liberties of this kind:

First: only *nature* can justify them. Hence they may
not be the product of choice or of deliberate imitation;
for we can never allow to a will that is always di-
rected according to moral laws the privilege of sensu-
ousness. (218) They must therefore be *naivety*. In
order, however, to convince us that they are truly so,
we must see them supported and accompanied by all
else that is likewise grounded in nature, for nature can
only be recognized by the rigorous consequence,
unity, and uniformity of her effects. Only to a heart
that despises all artificiality outright, and hence also
even if it is useful, do we permit its exemption where
it represses and limits; only to a heart that subordi-
nates itself to all the shackles of nature do we permit
that it make use of her freedom. All other feelings
of such a person must in consequence bear the im-
press of naturalness; he must be true, simple, free,
candid, full of feeling, upright; all deception, cunning,
all caprice, all petty selfishness must be banished from
his character, every trace of them from his work.

Second: only *beautiful* nature can justify liberties of this sort. Therefore they may not be onesided manifestations of appetite; for everything that originates in crude necessity is contemptible. From the totality and from the richness of human nature these sensuous energies must likewise derive. They must be *humanity*. But in order to be able to judge that the whole of human nature demands them and not merely a onesided and vulgar exigency of sensuousness, we must see that whole depicted of which they represent a single feature. In itself the sensuous mode of feeling is something innocent and indifferent. It displeases us in a human being only because it is animal and testifies to a lack of a more truly perfect humanity in him: it offends us in a work of art only because such a work makes a claim to please us and hence assumes that *we* are also capable of such a lack. But if we surprise in a person humanity functioning in all its remaining aspects, (219) if we find in the work in which liberties of this species have been exercised all the realities of mankind expressed, then that ground of our disapproval is removed and we can delight with unequivocal joy in the naive expression of true and beautiful nature. The same poet, therefore, who may allow himself to make us participants in such basely human feelings, must on the other hand be able to elevate all that is humanly great and beautiful and sublime.

This, then, would provide us with the criterion to which we could with certainty submit every poet who offends somewhat against propriety, and forces his freedom in the depiction of nature to this extreme. His work is vulgar and low, reprehensible without

exception, if it is *cold*, if it is *empty*, for this reveals
its origin in intention and in vulgar exigency, and is a
heinous assault on our appetites. On the other hand,
it is beautiful, noble, and worthy of applause despite
all the objections of frozen decency, if it is naive and
binds spirit and heart together.*

If I am told that, according to the criterion laid
down here, most French narratives of this genre and
their best imitations in Germany would not survive—
that this would in part be the case with many a prod-
uct of our most graceful and gifted poet, not even
excepting his masterpieces—to this I have no reply.
The dictum itself is anything but new, and I give here
the grounds of (220) a judgment which has already
long been enunciated by every finer feeling on this
subject. But these very principles which perhaps ap-
pear all too rigorous in connection with those writings
may perhaps be found too liberal in connection with
some other works; for I do not deny that the same
grounds on which I find entirely inexcusable the
seductive pictures of the Roman and German Ovid,
as well as of Crébillon, Voltaire, Marmontel (who
calls himself a moral narrator), Laclos, and many
others, yet reconcile me to the elegies of the Roman
and German Propertius, even to some of the ill-
reputed works of Diderot,[32] for the former are only

---

* And *heart:* for the merely sensuous ardor of the portrayal and
the luxuriant richness of imagination do not by far make it so.
Thus *Ardinghello* remains, despite all its sensuous energy and
all the fire of its coloration, only a sensuous caricature with-
out truth and without aesthetic dignity. Still, this unusual pro-
duction will always remain remarkable as an example of the
almost poetic impetus which *mere appetite* was capable of sup-
plying. [Translator's note: Wilhelm Heinse, *Ardinghello, or the
Enchanting Islands* (1787) was a contemporary "hit."]

witty, only prosaic, only lascivious, while the latter are poetic, human, and naive.*

Idyll

(221) There remain a few more words for me to say about this third species of sentimental poetry, a few words only, because a more detailed development of them, which they surely require, is reserved for another occasion.* [33]

* If I mention the immortal author of *Agathon, Oberon,* etc., in this company I must declare expressly that I do not mean to confuse him with them. His portrayals, even those most objectionable from this point of view, have no material tendency (as a recent, somewhat thoughtless, critic permitted himself to suggest not long ago); the author of *Love for Love* and of so many other naive and gifted works, in all of which the features of a beautiful and noble soul are unmistakable, could not possess such a tendency at all. But he seems to me to be pursued by the quite exceptional misfortune that portrayals of this kind are made necessary by the plan of his works. The cold understanding that designed that plan demanded them of him and his feeling seems to me so far removed from favoring them by preference that I believe I can still recognize that cold understanding in their execution. And this very coldness in depiction is damaging to them in judgment since only naive feeling can justify such portrayals aesthetically as well as morally. Whether the poet, however, is permitted in the designing of his plan to expose himself to such a danger in its execution, and whether a plan can be called poetic at all which, allowing the foregoing for the moment, cannot be executed without outraging the chaste feeling of the poet (221) as well as of the reader, and without forcing both to dwell on subjects from which refined feeling gladly retreats—this is what I doubt, and on which I would be glad to hear a reasonable opinion.

* I must repeat once again that satire, elegy, and idyll, as they are here laid down as the only three possible species of sentimental poetry, have nothing in common with the three particular genres of poem which are known by these names, other than the *modes of perception* which are proper to the former as well as to the latter. But that, beyond the limits of naive poetry,

The poetic representation of innocent and contented
mankind is the universal concept of this type of poetic
composition. Since this innocence and this contented-
ness appear incompatible with the artificial conditions
of society at large and with a certain degree of educa-
tion and refinement, the poets have removed the loca-
tion of idyll from the tumult of everyday life (223)
into the simple pastoral state and assigned its period
before the *beginnings of civilization* in the childlike
age of man. But one can readily grasp that these
designations are merely accidental, that they are not
to be considered as the purpose of the idyll, simply
as the most natural means to it. The purpose itself is
invariably only to represent man in a state of inno-

---

only this tripartite mode of perception and poetic composition
is possible, consequently that the area of sentimental poetry is
completely exhausted by this division, can be easily deduced
from the concept of the latter.

Sentimental is distinguished from naive poetry, namely, in
that it refers actual conditions, at which the latter halts, to
ideas, and applies ideas to actuality. Hence it has always, as
has already been observed above, to contend simultaneously
with two conflicting objects, i.e., with the ideal and with ex-
perience, between which neither more nor less than just these
three following relationships can be conceived of. Either it is
the *contradiction* with actual conditions, or it is its *correspond-
ence* with the ideal, which is the preferred attitude of mind, or
it is divided between the two. In the first case it is satisfied by
the force of the inner conflict, by *energetic movement;* in the
second, it is satisfied by the *harmony* of the inner life, by
dynamic calm; in the third, conflict *alternates* with harmony,
calm alternates with motion. This triadic state of feeling gives
rise to three different modes of poetry (222) to which the
customary names, *satire, idyll, elegy,* correspond exactly, pro-
vided only that one recalls the mood into which the poetic
species known by these names place the mind, and abstracted
from the means by which they achieve it.

Anyone who could now still ask me to which of the three

cence, i.e., in a condition of harmony and of peace with himself and with his environment.

But such a condition does not occur only before the beginnings of civilization, rather it is also the condition which civilization, if it can be said to have any particular tendency everywhere, aims at as its ultimate purpose. Only the idea of this condition and belief in its possible realization can reconcile man to all the evils to which he is subjected in the course of civilization, and were it merely a chimera the complaints of those would be justified who deplore society at large and the cultivation of the understanding simply as an evil, and assume that superseded state of nature to be the true purpose of mankind.[34] For the individual

---

species I assign the epic, the novel, the tragedy, etc., would not have understood me at all. For the concept of these last, as individual *genres of composition,* is either not at all or at least not solely determined by the mode of perception; it is clear, rather, that they can be executed in more than one mode of perception, consequently in more than one of the species of poetry I have established.

Finally, I have still to remark that if one is inclined to take sentimental poetry, as is reasonable, as a genuine order (and not simply as a degenerate species) and as an extension of true poetic art, then some attention must be paid to it in the determination of poetic types as well as generally in the whole of poetic legislation, which is still onesidedly based on the observances of the ancient and naive poets. The sentimental poet deviates too radically from the naive for those forms which the latter introduced to accommodate him at all times without strain. In such cases it is indeed difficult to distinguish correctly always the exceptions which the differentiation between the species demands, from the subterfuges to which incompetence resorts: but this much we learn from experience, that in the hands of sentimental poets (even the most outstanding) no single type of composition has ever remained entirely what it was among the ancients, and that often very new types have been executed under the old names.

who is immersed in civilization, infinitely much there-
fore depends upon his receiving a tangible assurance
of the realization of that idea in the world of sense,
of the possible reality of that condition, and since ac-
tual experience, far from nourishing this belief, rather
contradicts it constantly, here, as in so many cases, the
faculty of poetic composition comes to the aid of rea-
son in order to render that idea palpable to intuition
and to realize it in individual cases.

That innocence of the pastoral state is indeed also
a poetic conception, and hence imagination must al-
ready there have shown itself to be creative; but,
apart from the solution of the task having been incom-
parably simpler and easier, experience itself provided
the individual features from which it had only to
select and combine into (224) a whole. Beneath the
unclouded skies, in the simple conditions of the primi-
tive state, and with limited knowledge nature is easily
satisfied, and man does not become savage until dire
need has frightened him. All peoples who possess a his-
tory have a paradise, a state of innocence, a golden
age; indeed, every man has his paradise, his golden age,
which he recalls, according as he has more or less of
the poetic in his nature, with more or less inspiration.
Experience itself therefore supplies features enough
for the depiction of which the pastoral idyll treats. For
this reason it remains always a beautiful, an elevating
fiction, and the poetic power in representing it has
truly worked in behalf of the idea. For, to the man
who has once deviated from the simplicity of nature
and is delivered over to the dangerous guidance of his
reason, it is of infinite importance to perceive once
again nature's legislation in a pure exemplar, and in
this faithful mirror to be able once again to purify

himself of the corruption of civilization. But in doing so, one circumstance is involved that very much reduces the aesthetic value of such poems. Set *before the beginnings of civilization,* they exclude together with its disadvantages all its advantages, and by their very nature they find themselves necessarily in conflict with it. *Theoretically,* then, they lead us backwards, while *practically* they lead us forwards and ennoble us. Unhappily they place that purpose *behind* us, *toward* which they should, however, lead us, and hence they imbue us only with a sad feeling of loss, not with joyous feelings of hope. Since they can only attain their purpose by the denial of all art, and only by the simplification of human nature, they possess together with the utmost value for the *heart,* all too little for the *spirit,* and their narrow range is too soon exhausted. Therefore we can love them and seek them out when we stand in need of peace, but not when our (225) forces are striving for motion and activity. Only for the sick in spirit can they provide *healing,* but no *nourishment* for the healthy; they cannot unify, only assuage. This shortcoming grounded in the essence of the pastoral idyll has been beyond the art of the poets to correct. This type of composition has not, indeed, been lacking in enthusiastic admirers, and there are readers enough who can prefer an *Amyntas* and a *Daphnis* [35] to the greatest masterpieces of the epic and dramatic muses; but with such readers it is not so much their taste as their private needs that judges of works of art; consequently their opinion cannot be considered here. The reader of spirit and perception does not, indeed, mistake the value of such poetry, but he feels himself more rarely drawn to it and sooner satiated. They function at the needful mo-

ment all the more powerfully; but the truly beautiful
should not be obliged to wait for such a moment, but
should rather produce it.

What I am here criticizing in the bucolic idyll ap-
plies of course only to the sentimental; for the naive
can never be lacking content since here it is already
contained in the form itself. All poetry must indeed
possess an infinite content, only through this is it
poetry; but it can fulfill the requirement in two dif-
ferent ways. It can be infinite in accordance with its
form, if it presents its subject with *all its limits,* by
individualizing it; it can be infinite according to its
matter if it *removes all its limits* from the subject, by
idealizing it; hence either by an absolute representa-
tion or by the representation of an absolute. The naive
poet takes the first way, the sentimental the second.
The first cannot fall short of his content so long as he
remains faithful to nature which is always radically
limited, i.e., infinite in relation to its form. To this,
however, nature stands in opposition with her radical
limitation, since he should place an absolute (226)
content in the subject. The sentimental poet, there-
fore, does not well understand the advantages when
he *borrows his subjects* from the naive poet; in them-
selves they are completely indifferent and only be-
come poetic by their treatment. In this way he
imposes on himself a number of restrictions quite
unnecessarily, without power being able to carry
through the limitation completely, or to compete in
absolute assurance of the representation; he should
therefore rather remove himself in his subject from
the naive poet, because he can only regain from him
through the subject what the latter has to his advan-
tage in the form.

In order to make the application from this to the bucolic idyll of the sentimental poets, it now becomes clear why these poems, despite every effort of genius and art, are not completely satisfactory either for the heart or for the spirit. They implement an ideal, and yet retain the narrower indigent pastoral world, whereas they should absolutely have chosen either another world for the ideal, or a different representation for the pastoral world. They are so far ideal that thereby the representation loses in individual truth, yet again they are so far individual that the ideal content suffers thereby. One of Gessner's shepherds, for example, cannot delight us as nature by the fidelity of imitation, since for this he is too ideal a being; he can as little satisfy us as an ideal by infinitude of thought since for this he is much too inadequate a creature. He will, indeed, satisfy all classes of readers without exception up to a certain point because he strives to unite the naive with the sentimental, and consequently discharges to a certain degree the two opposed demands that can be made on a poem; but because the poet, in the effort to unify both, fails to do justice to either one, and is neither wholly nature (227) nor wholly ideal, he cannot for that very reason be quite acceptable to a rigorous taste that cannot forgive half-measures in aesthetic matters. It is extraordinary that this half-way state extends likewise to the language of the poet we have mentioned; he wavers undecided between poetry and prose, as though the poet were fearful of removing himself in metrical address too far from actual nature, and in nonmetrical address of losing his poetic impulse. A loftier satisfaction is aroused by Milton's superb representation of the first human couple and the state of

innocence in paradise: the most beautiful idyll known
to me of the sentimental type. Here nature is noble,
spirited, at once full of range and depth, the highest
meaning of humanity clothed in the most graceful
form.

Hence here too, in the idyll, as in all other poetic
types, one must make a choice once and for all be-
tween individuality and ideality; for to seek to satisfy
both demands simultaneously is, so long as one has
not reached the acme of perfection, the surest way of
falling short of both. Should the modern feel within
himself sufficient of the Greek spirit to compete, de-
spite all the intractability of his material, with the
Greek on his own ground, namely in the field of naive
poetry, then let him do it wholly and exclusively, and
liberate himself from every demand of the sentimental
taste of the age. He may indeed reach his model with
difficulty; between the original and the most successful
epigone a perceptible interval will always remain
open, but by these means he is nevertheless certain to
produce a genuinely poetic work.* If he is driven
(228) on the contrary, to the ideal by the sentimental
poetic impulse, then let him pursue this wholly, in
complete purity, and not rest content until he has
reached the highest, without looking back to see
whether actuality has borne him out. Let him despise

---

* Herr Voss has recently not only enriched our German litera-
ture with such a work, his *Luise,* but has also truly extended it.
This idyll, if not completely free of sentimental influences, does
belong wholly to the naive genre, and vies with rare success by
its individual truth and unalloyed nature with the best Greek
models. It cannot therefore (and this accrues (228) much to
its credit) be compared with any modern poem, but must be
compared with Greek models, with which it also shares the
exceedingly rare advantage of according us a pure, certain, and
always unmixed pleasure.

the unworthy evasion of cheapening the meaning of the ideal in order to accommodate it to human inadequacy, or of excluding the spirit in order to make readier way with the heart. Let him not lead us backwards into our childhood in order to secure to us with the most precious acquisitions of the understanding a peace which cannot last longer than the slumber of our spiritual faculties, but rather lead us forward into our maturity in order to permit us to perceive that higher harmony which rewards the combatant and gratifies the conqueror. Let him undertake the task of idyll so as to display that pastoral innocence even in creatures of civilization and under all the conditions of the most active and vigorous life, of expansive thought, of the subtlest art, the highest social refinement, which, in a word, leads man who cannot now go back to Arcady forward to Elysium.

The concept of this idyll is the concept of a conflict fully reconciled not only in the individual, but in society, of a free uniting of inclination with the law, of a nature illuminated by the highest moral dignity, briefly, none other than the ideal of beauty applied to actual life. Its character thus subsists in the complete reconciliation of *all opposition between actuality and the ideal* which has supplied material for satirical and elegiac poetry, and therewith (229) all conflict in the feelings likewise. Calm would then be the predominant impression of such a poetic type, but calm of perfection, not of inertia; a calm that derives from the balance not the arresting of those powers that spring from richness and not emptiness, and is accompanied by the feeling of an infinite capacity. But for the very reason that all resistance vanishes it will then be incomparably more difficult than in the two former

types of poetry to represent *motion*, without which,
however, no poetic effect whatsoever can be con-
ceived. The highest unity must prevail; but not at the
expense of variety; the mind must be satisfied, but not
so that aspiration ceases on that account. The resolu-
tion of this question is in fact what the theory of the
idyll has to supply.

[CONCLUSION OF THE TREATISE ON NAIVE AND SENTIMENTAL POETRY TOGETHER WITH SOME OBSERVATIONS CONCERNING A CHARACTERISTIC DIFFERENCE AMONG MEN (*Die Horen,* No. 1, 1796)]

The following has been established on the relation of
both modes of poetry to one another and to the
poetic ideal:

To the naive poet nature has granted the favor of
functioning always as an undivided unity, to be at
every instant an independent and complete whole, and
to represent mankind, in all its significance, in actu-
ality. Upon the sentimental poet she has conferred the
power, or rather impressed a lively impulse, to restore
out of himself that unity that has been disrupted by
abstraction, to complete the humanity within himself,
and from a limited condition to pass over into an in-
finite one.* (230) But to give human nature its full

* For the reader whose scrutiny is critical I add that both
modes of perception considered in their ultimate concepts are
related to one another like the first and third categories, in
that the last always arises by the combination of the first with
its exact opposite. The opposite of naive perception is, namely,

expression is the common task of both, and without
that they could not be called poets at all; the naive
poet, however, always possesses one advantage of sen-
suous reality over the sentimental, since he implements
as an actual fact what the other only strives to attain.
And this it is too that everyone experiences in himself
when he observes himself in the enjoyment of naive
poetry. He feels all the powers of his humanity active
in such a moment, he stands in need of nothing, he is
a whole in himself; without distinguishing anything in
his feeling, he is at once pleased with his spiritual ac-
tivity and his sensuous life. It is quite another mood
into which the sentimental poet casts him. Here he
feels only a lively *impulse* to produce that harmony in
himself which he there actually felt, to make a whole
of himself, to give complete expression to the human-
ity within himself. Hence in the latter his mind is in
motion, it is in tension, it wavers between conflicting
feelings; whereas in the former it is calm, relaxed, at
one with itself and completely satisfied.

But if the naive poet gains on the one hand in real-
ity at the expense of the sentimental, and brings into

---

reflective understanding, and the sentimental mood is the re-
sult of the effort, *even under the conditions of reflection,* to
restore naive feeling according to its content. (230) This
would occur through the fulfilled ideal in which art again
encounters nature. If one considers those three concepts in rela-
tion to the categories one will always find *nature* and the naive
mood corresponding to her in the first; *art,* as the antithesis of
nature by the freely functioning understanding, always in the
second; the *ideal,* in which consummated art always returns
to nature in the third category. [Translator's note: The refer-
ence here is to the Kantian categories which are generated in
triads in the way the argument is structured in all the major
essays of Schiller. Cf. § 11 in the *Critique of Pure Reason* on
the deduction of the categories.]

actual existence what the latter can only arouse a lively
impulse to attain, the latter for his part possesses the
great advantage over the first that he can give the
impulse a *greater object* (231) than the former has
supplied or could supply. All actuality, we know, falls
short of the ideal; everything existing has its limits, but
thought is boundless. From this limitation to which
everything sensuous is subjected, the naive poet there-
fore also suffers, whereas the unconditional freedom
of the faculty of ideas accrues to the sentimental. The
former therefore indeed fulfills his task, but the task
itself is something limited; the latter indeed does not
fulfill his, but his task is an infinite one. In this, too,
everyone can learn from his own experience. From the
naive poet one turns with facility and eagerness to the
active environment; the sentimental will always for a
few moments disaffect one for actual life. This is be-
cause our minds are here extended by the infinitude of
the idea beyond their natural circumscription, so that
nothing to hand can any longer be adequate to it. We
fall back rather, lost in our thoughts, where we find
nourishment for the impulse generated in the world of
ideas instead of seeking outside ourselves, as with the
former, for sensuous objects. Sentimental poetry is the
offspring of retreat and quietude, and to them, too, it
invites us; the naive is the child of life, and to life
also it leads us back.

I have called naive poetry a *favor of nature* to un-
derscore that reflection has no part in it. It is a lucky
throw of the dice, standing in no need of improvement
if successful, but equally incapable of any if it should
fail. In his feeling the whole work of the naive genius
is acquitted; here is his strength and his limit. If he
has not at once *felt* poetically, i.e., not at once com-

pletely humanly, then this shortcoming can no longer be repaired by art. Criticism can only afford him an insight into his mistake, but it cannot supply any beauty in its place. By his nature the naive genius must do everything; by his freedom he can achieve (232) little; and it will fulfill its essence so long as nature in him should operate according to an inner necessity. Now everything indeed is necessary that takes place by nature: this applies equally to every product of the naive genius (from whom nothing is farther removed than arbitrary action) be it never so successful; but the coercion of the moment is one thing, the inner necessity of the whole quite another. Considered as a whole, nature is independent and infinite; in any individual manifestation, however, she is dependent and limited. This, therefore, applies also to the nature of the poet. Even the most felicitous moment in which he can find himself is dependent upon a preceding one; hence, too, only a conditional necessity can be attributed to him. But now the poet is assigned the task of equating an individual state to the human whole, consequently to base that state absolutely and necessarily upon himself. Hence, every trace of temporal dependence must be removed from the moment of inspiration, and the subject itself, however limited it may be, may not limit the poet. It will be readily understood that this is possible only insofar as the poet brings to the subject absolute freedom and breadth of ability and as he is practised in embracing everything with his whole humanity. His practice, however, he can receive only from the world in which he lives and by which he is directly affected. The naive genius is thus dependent upon experience in a way unknown to the sentimental. The latter, we know,

(sentimental)

only begins his function where the former concludes his; his strength subsists in completing an inadequate subject *out of himself* and by his own power to transform a limited condition into a condition of freedom. Thus the naive poetic genius requires assistance from without, whereas the sentimental nourishes and purifies himself from within; around him he must observe nature instinct with form, a poetic world, naive humanity, since it must (233) complete its work in sense perception. If, however, this assistance from without is not forthcoming, he finds himself surrounded by a spiritless matter, and only two things then occur. Either he abandons his species if the genus predominates in him, and he becomes sentimental if only to remain poetic; or, if the characteristics of the species retain their predominance, he abandons his genus and becomes common nature if only to remain nature. The first may well be the case with the finest sentimental poets in the ancient Roman world and in more modern times. Had they been born in another age, transplanted beneath other skies, they, who now move us by ideas, would have enchanted us by individual truth and naive beauty. From the second the poet could only with difficulty protect himself if he cannot abandon nature in a vulgar world.

Actual nature, of course; but from this one cannot carefully enough distinguish *true* nature which is the *subject* of naive poetry. Actual nature exists everywhere, but true nature is all the rarer, for to it belongs an inner necessity of existence. Actual nature is every outburst of passion, however crude; it may even be true nature, but truly *human* it cannot be, for this requires some participation of the independent faculties in every utterance the expression of which is to possess dignity. Actual human nature includes every moral baseness, but it is to be hoped that true human nature does not; for the latter cannot be other than noble. The absurdities cannot be overlooked to which this confusion between actual and true human nature has misled criticism as well as practice: what trivialities have been permitted, even praised, in poetry because, alas! they are actual nature; how pleased one is to find caricatures which are ghastly enough in the actual world carefully transported into the poetic and counterfeited true to life. Certainly, (234) the poet may imitate bad nature also, and indeed the very notion of satire involves this: but in this case his own beautiful nature must be conveyed with the subject, but the vulgar material must not drag the imitator down with it. If only he himself is true human nature at least in the moment of execution then it does not matter at all what he executes: but equally we can only accept a true picture of actuality from the hands of such a poet. Woe unto us readers, if the grotesque mirrors itself in the grotesque, if the scourge of satire falls into the hands of one whom nature intended should wield a much more serious lash, if men who, devoid of everything that one can call poetic spirit, possess only the apish talent of vulgar imitation and exercise it in a gruesome and frightful manner at the expense of our taste!

But even for the truly naive poet, I have noted, common nature can become dangerous; for in the final analysis that fine accord between feeling and thinking in which his character subsists, is still only an idea that is never entirely attained in actuality; and even in the most fortunate geniuses of this class, passive receptivity is always more or less dependent upon external impression and only a continuous agility of the productive faculties, which is not to be expected of human nature, would be able to prevent the material from exercising upon occasion its blind power over receptivity. Whenever this is the case, poetic feeling turns into the vulgar.*

* How very much the naive poet is dependent upon his subject and how much, even everything, depends upon his feelings, the ancient poetic art can supply us with the best examples. To the extent that nature within and without them is beautiful, the poetry of the ancients is likewise so; but if, on the contrary, nature is vulgar, then the spirit has (235) fled from their poetry. Every reader of finer feeling must sense, for example, in their depictions of feminine nature, of the relation between the two sexes and of love in particular, a certain emptiness and satiety that all the truth and naivety of the representation cannot overcome. Without speaking of fanatical enthusiasm which, of course, does not ennoble nature but detracts from it, one may, it is to be hoped, assume that in reference to that relationship of the sexes and the passion of love nature is capable of a nobler character than the ancients gave it; we know too of the *incidental* circumstances which for them stood as an obstacle to the refinement of those feelings. That it was narrowness, not inner necessity, that kept the ancients at a lower level is shown by the example of the modern poets who have gone so much further than their predecessors, still without exceeding the bounds of nature. Here we are not speaking of that which sentimental poets have made of this subject, for they do go beyond nature into the ideal, and, therefore, their example cannot be applied against the ancients; but we are speaking of the manner in which this subject has been treated by truly naive poets as, for example, in the *Sakuntala,* by the minnesingers in many a courtly tale and knightly epic, or by Shakespeare, Fielding, and many others, even by German poets. This would then have provided the occasion for the ancients to spiritualize from within themselves a theme which externally was too crude to supply the poetic meaning, which was lacking in external perception, by means of reflection, to supplement nature by the idea; in a word, to make a limited object into an infinite one by a sentimental operation. But these were naive, not sentimental, poetic geniuses; their work was, therefore, terminated with the external perception. [Translator's note: *Sakuntala:* a Sanskrit drama of the first century B.C. by Kalidasa, known to Schiller in the translation by Johann Forster (1791).]

(235) No genius of the naive category, from Homer down to Bodmer,[36] has entirely avoided these reefs; but of course they are most dangerous to those who are obliged to defend themselves externally from vulgar nature, or whose inner cultivation is destroyed by a lack of discipline. The first is responsible for the fact that even cultivated writers do not (236) always remain free of platitudes, and the second that many a fine talent is prevented from occupying the rank to which nature has called it. The comic poet, whose genius most of all is nourished by actual life, is for that very reason most exposed to platitude, as indeed the examples of Aristophanes and Plautus and of almost all the later poets show who have followed in their footsteps. How long does even the sublime Shakespeare let us sink sometimes; with what trivialities are we not tormented by Lope de Vega, Molière, Regnard, Goldoni; into what mire are we not dragged down by Holberg? Schlegel, one of the most gifted poets of our fatherland, whose genius could not but shine among the foremost in this category; Gellert, a truly naive poet, as also Rabener, even Lessing, the cultivated student of criticism and a so watchful judge of his own work—do they not all, more or less, pay for the insipid character of the nature they have selected as the material of their satire? I do not mention any of the most recent writers of this class since there are none that I can except.[37]

And not enough that the naive poetic spirit is in danger of nourishing itself all too much with common reality—by the facility with which it expresses itself, and precisely by means of this greater assimilation to actual life it encourages the vulgar imitator to try his hand in the realm of poetry. Sentimental poetry, albeit

dangerous enough from another point of view, as I
shall later show, at least keeps *these* folk at a distance,
because it is not everyone's forte to elevate himself to
the idea; but naive poetry bears within itself the belief
that it is mere feeling, mere humor, mere imitation of
actual nature that makes for the poet. But nothing is
more repellent than the banal individual who takes it
into his head to be ingratiating and naive—he who
should envelop himself in all the veils of art in order
to conceal his (237) loathsome nature. From this
source, too, come the unspeakable platitudes which
Germans love to hear in the form of naive and comic
songs and with which they are wont to amuse them-
selves incessantly at a well-laden table. Granted the
license of whimsy, of feeling, these paltry things are
tolerated—but this whimsy and this feeling cannot
be too carefully suppressed. The muses on the Pleisse
constitute a specially pitiful chorus in this respect, and
they are answered in no better accords by the Thalias
of the Leine and Elbe.*[38] These jokes are as insipid as
the passion is pitiful that is heard upon our tragic stages
and that, instead of imitating true nature, achieves

* These gentle friends have received very unkindly what a
reviewer in the *Allgemeine Literatur-Zeitung* criticized a few
years ago in Bürger's poems, and the spite with which they
lick at this thorn seems to be an acknowledgment that with
the cause of this poet they believe that they are contesting
their own. But in this they are much in error. That censure
could only apply to a true poetic genius, richly endowed by
nature, but who had failed by his own education to cultivate
that rare gift. Such an individual ought to and must be sub-
jected to the highest criteria of art, because he possesses the
power, if only he seriously intended to be equal to it; but it
would be at once ridiculous and cruel to proceed in like man-
ner with people whom nature has not favored, and who in
every work they place upon the market display a completely
convincing (238) certificate of indigence.

only the spiritless and ignoble expression of the actual, so that after such a tearful dish we are in the same mood as if we had just paid a visit to a hospital or read Salzmann's *Human Misery*.[39] Matters are still worse with satiric poetry and particularly with the comic novel which simply by its nature is so close to common life and hence ought, like any frontier post, to be in the safest hands. That man is truly least called to be (238) the *portrayer* of his times who is its *creature* and its *caricature*; but because it is so easy to conjure up some kind of comic character from one's own acquaintance, even if only *a fat man*,[40] and to get the grotesque down on paper with a crude pen, even the sworn enemies of everything in the poetic spirit sometimes feel the urge to flounder in this style and delight a circle of worthy friends with the fair offspring. A purely attuned feeling would, of course, never be in danger of confusing these products of a vulgar nature with the gifted fruits of naive genius; but it is precisely this mode of pure feeling that is lacking, and in most cases the attempt is made only to gratify a desire without making any demands on the spirit. The so patently misunderstood notion, true enough in itself, that one finds *recreation* in works of *bel esprit*, contributes substantially to this indulgence, if one can indeed call it indulgence when nothing loftier is intimated and the reader profits by it in the same manner as the author. Common nature, in fact, when it is under tension, can only recuperate in emptiness, and even a higher degree of understanding, if it is not supported by an equivalent cultivation of feeling, relaxes from its affairs only in insipid sensual enjoyment.

If the poetic genius must elevate itself by its free individual activity above all *accidental* limits that are

inseparable from any *determined* condition in order to
attain to human nature in its absolute capacity, it may
not, on the other hand, go beyond the *necessary* limits
which are involved in the concept of human nature;
for the absolute (but only within humanity) is its task
and its sphere. We have seen that the naive genius is
not in fact in danger of surpassing this sphere, nor like-
wise (239) of *exhausting it fully,* if it sets external
necessity or the accidental exigency of the moment too
much in the place of inner necessity. The sentimental
genius, however, is exposed to the danger, due to the
effort of removing all limitations from it, of suppressing
human nature altogether, and not only, as it may and
should, elevating or *idealizing* it above and beyond all
determined and limited actuality to absolute possibil-
ity, but rather of going still further beyond possibility
or otherwise falling into extravagant *enthusiasm.* This
error of *overtension* is as much founded in a specific
idiosyncrasy of its procedure as the opposed idea of
indolence is the idiosyncratic approach of the naive.
For the naive genius permits nature to reign unre-
strictedly within himself, and since nature in its indi-
vidual temporal manifestations is always dependent
and scanty, naive feeling will not always remain suffi-
ciently *exalted* to be able to resist the accidental de-
termination of the moment. On the other hand, the
sentimental genius abandons actuality in order to rise
upward to ideas and to command his material with free
spontaneity; but since reason, in accordance with its
laws, always strives toward the unconditioned, the
sentimental genius will not always remain sufficiently
dispassionate to maintain himself uninterruptedly and
uniformly within the conditions that are entailed in the
concept of human nature and to which reason, even in

its freest effects, must here always remain bound. This could take place only through a relative degree of receptivity which, however, in the sentimental spirit, is as far outweighed by spontaneity as in the naive it outweighs spontaneity. If one therefore sometimes misses the spirit in the creations of naive genius, one will frequently seek in vain in the products of the sentimental for the matter. Both, therefore, albeit in entirely opposed (240) ways, fall into the error of *emptiness*; for matter without spirit, and a play of spirit without matter, are both a cipher in the aesthetic judgment.

All poets who draw their material too onesidedly from the world of thought and are driven more by an inner wealth of ideas than by stress of feeling to the poetic image are more or less in danger of falling into this bypath. In its creations reason draws too little upon this counsel of the limits of the sensuous world, and thought is always driven farther than experience can follow. If, however, it is driven so far that not only could no particular experience correspond to it (for thus far the ideally beautiful may and must go), but rather that it in fact contravenes the conditions of all possible experience and consequently, in order to make it actual, human nature would have to be totally and completely abandoned, then such a thought is no longer poetic but overstrained—provided, however, that it has declared itself as representable and poetic; for if it does not possess this it would still suffice if it only does not contradict itself. If it does contradict itself it is no longer overstrain, but *nonsense;* for that which does not exist at all can likewise not exceed its boundaries. If, however, it should not declare itself as an object for the imagination then, too, it is not overstrained; for mere thought is boundless, and whatever

has no limits cannot surpass any. Hence only that can
be called overstrained that outrages, not indeed logi-
cal, but sensuous truth, while still making claims upon
it. If, then, a poet has the unhappy inspiration of
choosing as a theme for depiction natures that are
simply *superhuman* and which also *may* not be repre-
sented otherwise, he cannot save himself from being
overstrained by abandoning the poetic and by not even
undertaking to allow his subject to be executed by the
imagination. For if he were to do this, (241) either it
would carry over its own limits to the subject, and
make of an absolute object a limited *human* one (as,
for example, all the Greek gods are, and rightly so), or
the subject would remove the limits set to imagination,
i.e., it would suppress them, and in this precisely the
overstrain subsists.

Overstrain in feeling must be distinguished from
overstrain in representation; we are speaking here only
of the first. The object in perception can be unnatural,
but in itself is nature, and hence must speak in her own
behalf. If, therefore, overstrain in feeling can flow out
of warmheartedness and a truly poetic disposition,
then overstrain in representation testifies always to a
cold heart, and very often to poetic incapacity. It is
therefore not a mistake against which the sentimental
poetic genius might have to be warned, but which
threatens only his uninspired imitator, especially since
he does not disdain the company of the banal, insipid,
and even base. Overstrained feeling is by no means
without truth, and as actual feeling it must also neces-
sarily possess a real object. Because it is nature it also
admits of simple expression and, coming from the
heart, it cannot fail to reach the heart. Since its subject
is not drawn from nature but is onesidedly and artifi-

cially advanced by the understanding, it possesses a too merely logical reality, and the feeling is therefore not purely human. It is not an illusion that Héloise feels for Abélard, Petrarch for his Laura, St. Preux for his Julie, Werther for his Lotte, and what Agathon, Phanias, Peregrinus Proteus (Wieland's, I mean) feel for their ideals.[41] The feeling is true, but its object is artificial and lies outside human nature. If their feeling had simply remained attached to the sensuous truth of its objects it would (242) not have been able to assume that impetus; on the other hand a merely capricious play of fantasy without any inner meaning would likewise not have been able to touch our hearts, for the heart is touched only by reason. This overstrain, then, merits correction, not contempt, and whoever mocks at it should ask himself whether he is not perhaps so clever out of heartlessness, or so cautious out of lack of reason. Thus the exaggerated tenderness in matters of gallantry and honor that characterizes the knightly romances, particularly the Spanish, the scrupulous delicacy driven to the point of preciosity in the French and English sentimental novels (of the best kind) are not only subjectively true, but also, objectively considered, not without substance; they are genuine feelings actually derived from a moral source and are only objectionable because they surpass the bounds of human truth. Without that moral reality how would it be possible that they could be communicated with such power and fervor as we nonetheless find them in experience to be? The same applies also to moral and religious enthusiasm and to exalted love of freedom and fatherland. Since the objects of these feelings are always ideas and do not appear in external experience (for what affects the political enthusiast, for example, is not what he sees, but what he thinks), the spontaneous imagination possesses a dangerous freedom and cannot, as in other cases, be restored to its limits by the sensuous presence of its objects. But neither man in general nor the poet in particular may withdraw himself from the jurisdiction of nature other than to submit to the opposed jurisdiction of reason; only for the ideal may he abandon actuality, since by one of these two anchors freedom *must* be secured. But the path from experience to the ideal is long, and in between lies fantasy with unbridled fortuitousness. It is therefore (243) unavoidable that man in general, just as the poet in particular, if he should quit the domination of feeling for the freedom of his understanding without having been driven to it by the laws of reason, i.e., if he leaves nature through caprice, then he will remain *without a law*, and is thus rendered up a prey to the fantastic.

Experience shows that whole peoples as well as individuals who have withdrawn from the secure guidance of nature are actually in this state, and this too provides sufficient examples of an analogous deviation in the art of poetry. Because the genuine sentimental poetic impulse must, in order to elevate itself to the idea, pass beyond the limits of actual nature, the inauthentic goes beyond every limit whatever and persuades itself that the mere wild play of imagination is all that makes for poetic inspiration. To the true poetic genius, who abandons actuality only for the sake of the idea, this can either never happen, or only in those moments in which he has lost himself; yet he, on the other hand, can be seduced by his own nature into an exaggerated mode of perception. He can, however, seduce others into the fantastic by his example, because readers of vivid fantasy and weak understanding take into account only the license against actual nature which he permits himself, without being able to follow him as far as his lofty inner necessity. The same thing happens here to the sentimental genius that we have observed in the naive. Since the latter carries out by his nature everything that he does, the vulgar imitator prefers no worse guide than his own nature. Masterpieces of the naive category will, therefore, usually have as their sequel the most banal and sordid impressions of vulgar nature, and the chief works of the sentimental genre, a numerous host of fantastic productions; and this can easily be demonstrated in the literature of every people.

With reference to poetry, two principles are (244) employed which in themselves are completely correct, but in the interpretation in which they are commonly taken, cancel one another out. Of the first: "That the art of poetry serves for pleasure and recreation," we have already observed that it not a little favors emptiness and platitude in poetic depictions; by the second principle: "That it serves for the moral ennoblement of man," the exaggerated finds protection. It is not superfluous to illuminate somewhat more closely both these principles, which are so often enunciated, so often incorrectly interpreted, and so clumsily applied.

By recreation we mean the transition from an intense state to one which is natural to us. Everything here, of course, depends on what we posit our natural condition to be, and what we understand by an intense one. If we posit the former exclusively in an unbridled play of the physical powers, and in liberty from every constraint, then all activity of reason (because it exercises resistance to sensuousness) becomes a violence done to us, and spiritual quietude combined with sensuous activity is the proper ideal of recreation. If, however, we posit our natural condition as an unlimited capacity for every human utterance, and in the ability to exercise all our powers with equal freedom, then any separation and *isolation* of these powers is an intense condition, and the ideal of recreation is the restoration of our whole nature after onesided tensions. The first ideal is therefore dictated solely by the needs of *sensuous* nature, the second by the independence of *human* nature. Which of these two types of recreation the art of poetry ought and must supply can scarcely be a question in theory; for no one would gladly give the appearance that he could be tempted to set the ideal of humanity beneath the ideal of animality. (245) Nevertheless, the demands that one is accustomed in actual life to make of poetic works are drawn by preference from the sensuous ideal and in most cases in accordance with it—not indeed the *esteem* determined that one accords to these works, but certainly the *predilection* is decided and the *favorite* chosen. The state of mind of most people is on the one hand intensive and exhausting *labor,* on the other, enervating *indulgence.* The former, we know, renders the sensuous need for spiritual calm and for cessation of activity unequally more pressing than the moral need for harmony and for an absolute freedom of function, because above all else *nature* must be satisfied before the *mind* can make its demands; the latter confines and cripples the moral impulses themselves which that demand must give rise to. Hence nothing is more disadvantageous for sensitivity to the truly beautiful than both these all-too-common frames of mind among men, and from this it becomes clear why so few, even among better men, possess correct judgment in aesthetic matters. Beauty is the product of accord between the mind and the senses; it addresses itself at once to all the faculties of man and can, therefore, be perceived and appreciated only under the condition that he employ all his powers fully and freely. One must assemble clear senses, a full heart, a fresh and unimpaired mind, one's whole nature must be collected, which is by no means the case with those who are divided in themselves by abstract thought, hemmed in by petty business formalities, or exhausted by strenuous concentration. These persons yearn indeed for sensuous matter, but not in order to stop it. They want to be free, but only from a burden that fatigues their lassitude, not from a barrier that blocks their activity.

(246) Should one then still be amazed at the happiness of mediocrity and emptiness in aesthetic matters, or at the vengeance of weak minds upon the truly and actively beautiful? They expected recreation from it, but a recreation to meet their need and in accordance with their feeble notion, and they discover with dismay that they are now first expected to put out an effort of strength for which they might lack the capacity even in their best moments. There, on the contrary, they are welcome as they are; for as little strength as they bring with them, still they need very much less to exhaust the minds of their writers. Here they are at once relieved of the burden of thought; and nature relaxed can indulge itself upon the downy pillow of *platitude* in blessed enjoyment of nothingness. In the temple of Thalia and Melpomene,[42] as it is established among us, the beloved goddess sits enthroned receiving in her ample bosom the dull pedant and the tired

businessman, and lulls the mind into a mesmeric sleep, thawing out the frigid senses and rocking the imagination in gentle motion.

And why should one not indulge vulgar individuals, when that is often enough done for the best ones? The relaxation that nature demands after every sustained effort and also takes without invitation (and only for such moments does one reserve the enjoyment of beautiful works), is so little favorable to aesthetic judgment that among those classes who are really occupied only extremely few will be found who can judge in matters of taste with certainty, and what is here more to the point, with consistency. Nothing is more usual than that scholars, in contrast to cultivated mundane individuals, reveal themselves in judgments of beauty in the most ridiculous light, and in particular the critics of the plastic arts are the scorn of all connoisseurs. Their neglected, sometimes exaggerated, sometimes coarse, feeling leads them astray in most cases, (247) and even if they have seized upon something in theory in defence of it, they can only formulate *theoretical* (concerning the purposiveness of a work) not *aesthetic* judgments which must always comprehend the whole, and in which, therefore, feeling must decide. If they at last voluntarily renounce the latter and rest content with the former, they may yet be of sufficient use, since the poet in his inspiration and the perceptive reader at the moment of enjoyment may only too easily overlook details. But it is an all the more laughable spectacle if these crude natures who, with all their painstaking efforts at best attain to the cultivation of a single skill, set up their paltry personalities as representative of universal feeling, and in the sweat of their brows pass judgment upon the beautiful.

The concept of *recreation*, which poetry is to pro-
vide is, as we have seen, usually beset by too narrow
limits because one is accustomed to referring it too
onesidedly to mere crude necessity. The notion of *en-
noblement*, which the poet is supposed to aim at, is
exactly the reverse, because it is too onesidedly deter-
mined by the mere idea.

For, in accordance with the idea, ennoblement
passes always into the infinite because reason in its
demands is not bound by the necessary limits of the
world of sense and does not stop short of the abso-
lutely perfect. Nothing about which something still
higher can be conceived can satisfy it; at its stern
court no limitation of finite nature is acceptable in
excuse; it acknowledges no other boundaries but those
of thought, and of this we know that it soars beyond
all the limits of space and time. Such an ideal of en-
noblement which reason prescribes in its pure legisla-
tion may no more be established as his purpose by the
poet as that base ideal of recreation which (248) sen-
suousness sets up, since he should indeed liberate man-
kind from all accidental limitations, but without setting
aside its concept or disrupting its necessary limitations.
Whatever he allows himself beyond those limitations
is exaggeration, and it is to just this that he is all too
readily misled by a falsely construed concept of en-
noblement. But the evil is that he can scarcely elevate
himself to the true ideal of human ennoblement with-
out in any case taking a few steps beyond it. For in
order to attain to it he must abandon actuality, since
he can draw upon it, as upon any ideal, only out of
inner and moral sources. Not in the world that sur-
rounds him nor in the tumult of everyday life, but
only in his heart is it to be encountered, and only in

the stillness of solitary contemplation can he find his heart. Yet this withdrawal from life will not only remove from his vision the accidental limitations of mankind—it will often remove the necessary and insurmountable limitations, and in seeking the pure form he stands in danger of losing the entire meaning. Reason will pursue its business much too isolated from experience, and whatever the contemplative spirit has discovered in the serene course of thought, the man of action will not be able to realize in the tempestuous course of daily life. Thus the very same produces the fanatic that was solely able to engender the sage, and the advantage of the latter may perhaps subsist less in that he did not become the former than that he did not remain so.

It may therefore be left neither to the laboring classes of mankind to determine the concept of recreation in accordance with their needs, nor to the contemplative classes to determine the concept of ennoblement in accordance with their speculation. If the former concept is not to become too physical and too unworthy of poetry, nor the latter too hyperphysical and too extravagant for poetry—but both these concepts (249) as experience shows, govern common opinion of poetry and poetic works—then, in order to interpret it, we must look for a class of men which, without toiling, is active and capable of formulating ideals without fanaticism; a class that unites within itself all the realities of life with its least possible limitations and is borne by the current of events without becoming its victim. Only such a class can preserve the beautiful unity of human nature that is destroyed for the moment by any particular task, and continuously by a life of such toil, and decide, in everything that is purely human, by their *feelings* the rule of common opinion. Whether such a class might actually exist, or rather whether it actually does exist, given both the external conditions described and the inner disposition corresponding to the concept, is another question which I am not concerned with here. If it does not correspond to it, then it has only itself to blame, since the contrasting laboring class has at least the satisfaction of considering itself a victim of its labor. In such a class of society (which, however, I offer here only as an idea and by no means wish to have taken as a fact) the naive character would be united with the sentimental so that each would preserve the other from its own extreme, and while the first would save the mind from exaggerations the second would secure it against inertia. For, in the final analysis, we must nonetheless concede that neither the naive nor the sentimental character, each considered alone, quite exhausts that ideal of beautiful humanity that can only arise out of the intimate union of both.

For so long as one exalts both characters as far as the *poetic,* as we have thus far considered, much of the limitation which adheres to them falls away, and their antithesis becomes all the less noticeable the higher the degree to which they become poetic; for the poetic mood is an independent whole in which all distinctions and all shortcomings vanish. But (250) for the very reason that it is only the concept of the poetic in which both modes of perception can coincide, their mutual differences and interdependence become in the same degree more noticeable the more they are divested of their poetic character; and this is the case in ordinary life. The more they descend to this the more they lose of their generic character and they are brought closer until finally in their caricatures only their typological character remains to oppose one to the other.

[Human Types]

This leads me to a very remarkable psychological antagonism among men in a century that is civilizing itself: an antagonism that because it is radical and based on inner mental dispositions is the cause of an aggravated cleavage among men worse than any fortuitous clash of interests could ever provoke; one that deprives the artist and poet of all hope of pleasing and affecting universally, as is his task; which makes it impossible for the philosopher, even when he has done his utmost, to convince universally: yet the very concept of philosophy demands this; which, finally, will never permit a man in practical life to see his course of action universally approved—in a word, an antithesis that is to blame that no work of the spirit and no action of the heart can decisively satisfy one class without for that very reason bringing upon itself the damning judgment of the other. This antithesis is without doubt as old as the beginnings of civilization and is scarcely to be overcome before its end other than in a few rare individuals who, it is to be hoped, always existed and always will; but among its effects is also this one, that it defeats every effort to overcome it because neither side can be induced to admit that there is any shortcoming on its part and any reality on the other; despite this, it still remains profitable enough to pursue so important a cleavage back to its ultimate source and thereby to reduce the actual (251) point of the conflict at least to a simpler formulation.

One can best discover the true concept of this antithesis, as I have just remarked, by abstracting from both the naive and the sentimental character what each possesses of the poetic. From the first, then, nothing remains (from the theoretical point of view) but a sober spirit of observation and a fixed loyalty to the uniform testimony of the senses, and (from the practical point of view) a resigned submission to the necessity (but not the blind necessity) of nature: an accession thus to what is and what must be. Of the sentimental character nothing remains (theoretically) but a restless spirit of speculation that presses on to the unconditioned in all its knowledge, and (practically) a moral rigorism that insists upon the unconditioned in acts of the will. The member of the first class can be called a *realist* and of the other class an *idealist;* but these names should not recall either the good or bad senses which are connected with them in metaphysics.*

(252) Since the realist allows himself to be determined by the necessity of nature and the idealist by the necessity of reason, the same relation must obtain between them as is found between the effects of nature and the actions of reason. Nature, we know, although

---

* I note, in order to forestall any misunderstanding, that this division is by no means undertaken in order to promote a choice between them or therewith the preference of one to the exclusion of the other. It is just this *exclusion* which is found in experience that I am combatting; and the result of the present observations will be the proof that only by completely equal *inclusion* of both can justice be done to the rational concept of mankind. Moreover, I take both in their most dignified sense and in the whole wealth of their connotations which can only subsist together with their purity and the retention of their specific differences. It will also be apparent that a high degree of human truth is compatible with each and that their diversion from one another may indeed make a difference in detail but not in the whole; in the form perhaps, but not in the content.

of infinite dimension as a whole, displays its dependence and indigence in every particular manifestation; only in the universe of its phenomena does it express an independently vast character. Every particular within it subsists only because something else exists; nothing arises out of itself, everything springs out of the antecedent moment in order to give rise to the following one. But it is just this reciprocal relation of phenomena to one another that assures to each its existence by the existence of the other, and its constancy and necessity is inseparable from the dependence of its manifestations. Nothing is free in nature, but nothing is arbitrary in her either.

And in just this way the realist also reveals himself in his *knowledge* as well as in his *actions*. The compass of his knowledge and functions extends to everything that conditionally exists; but he can never proceed beyond conditional cognition, and the rules which he formulates out of particular experience apply, in their strictest form, only once also; but should he elevate the rule of the moment into a universal law he will irremediably fall into error. If, therefore, the realist seeks to attain to something unconditional in his knowledge, he must attempt to do so along the very same path by which nature becomes an absolute, that is, by the path of totality and in the universe of experience.

But since the sum of experience is never completely concluded, only a comparative totality is the highest to which the realist attains in his knowledge. He founds his insights upon the recurrence that fits into a law; but in whatever presents itself for the first (253) time, his wisdom returns to its beginnings.

Whatever applies to the realist's knowledge applies equally to his moral actions. His character possesses

morality, but this lies, considered according to its con-
cept, not in any particular act, but only in the whole
sum of his life. In every particular case he will be de-
termined by external causes and by external purposes;
but those causes will not be accidental nor those pur-
poses momentary, but will rather flow subjectively out
of the whole of nature and will refer back objectively
to it. Thus the impulses of his will are not, in the rigor-
istic sense, sufficiently free or morally pure enough,
because they have as their cause something other than
the pure will, and as their object something other than
pure law; yet these are by no means blind and materi-
alistic impulses since that something other is the abso-
lute totality of nature, and therewith something inde-
pendent and necessary. In this way common human
understanding, the most distinctive feature of the real-
ist, shows that it is universal in thought and conduct.
From the individual case he draws the rule of his judg-
ment, out of an inner perception the rule of his con-
duct; but by a happy instinct he is able to distinguish
from both everything that is momentary and inciden-
tal. By this method he proceeds excellently on the
whole, and will scarcely have to accuse himself of sig-
nificant errors; but he will not be able to lay claim to
greatness and dignity in any particular case. This is
the prize only of independence and freedom and in his
individual actions we see too few traces of these.

   With the idealist the situation is quite different; he
finds his cognitions and motives in himself and in pure
reason. If nature always appears dependent and lim-
ited in her individual manifestations, reason on the
other hand imposes the character of independence and
perfection equally in every individual action. It draws
everything out of itself, and to itself (254) it refers

everything. Whatever happens because of it happens
only for its sake; every concept that it establishes is an
absolute dimension, as is every decision that it formu-
lates. And the idealist reveals himself in the same way,
so far as he justly bears the name, in his knowledge as
in his actions. Dissatisfied with cognitions that are
valid only under certain presuppositions he seeks to
penetrate to truths for which no presuppositions are
necessary and which are the presuppositions of every-
thing else. He is satisfied only by the philosophical in-
sight that refers all conditional knowledge to the un-
conditional and attaches all experience to the necessary
in the human spirit; those things to which the realist
subordinates his thought, the idealist subordinates to
his faculty of thought. And in this he proceeds with
complete authority, for if the laws of the human spirit
were not simultaneously the laws of the universe; if
reason, in the last analysis, did not itself belong to
experience, then no experience would be possible
either.

But he can have reached as far as absolute truths
and yet still not be much furthered in knowledge
thereby. For while it is true that everything is subject
to necessary and universal laws, yet every individual
matter is governed by accidental and particular rules;
and in nature everything is individual. With his philo-
sophical cognition he can therefore command the
whole, while having gained nothing thereby for the
particular or in practice: indeed, because he every-
where penetrates to the *remote* causes by which every-
thing is possible, he can easily overlook the *proximate*
causes whereby everything becomes actual; because he
directs his attention in everything to the universal that
finds the common factor in the most varied instances,

he can easily neglect the particularity that differentiates them. He will, therefore, be able to *comprehend* very much by his knowledge and, perhaps for that very reason, *apprehend* very little, and often lose in insight what he gains in perspective. Thus it happens that if speculative understanding scorns (255) common sense for its *narrowness*, common understanding derides the speculative for its *emptiness*; for cognitions always lose in specific content what they gain in range.

In moral judgments one will find in the idealist a purer morality in individual matters, but much less uniformity as a whole. He is called an idealist only insofar as he takes the grounds of his determinations from pure reason, but reason displays itself in each of its utterances absolutely, hence his individual actions, if they are moral at all, will bear the *whole* character of moral independence and freedom; and if in actual life a truly moral deed could be found at all which would remain so even in face of rigorous scrutiny, then it could only be executed by the idealist. But the purer the morality of his individual actions the more fortuitous they are too, since consistency and necessity are indeed the character of nature, but not of freedom. Not, of course, that idealism could ever be in conflict with morality (which would be a contradiction in terms), but because human nature is simply incapable of strict idealism. If the realist, even in his moral actions, calmly and uniformly submits to physical necessity, the idealist requires inspiration, he must for the moment exalt his nature, for he can do nothing unless he is enthused. But then, of course, he can do all the more and his behavior will manifest a character of loftiness and grandeur which one looks for in vain in the actions of the realist. But actual life is by no means

fitted to arouse that enthusiasm in him and still less so
to maintain it uniformly. Set against the absolute great-
ness from which he always departs, the absolute small-
ness of the individual case to which he has to apply it
makes far too great a contrast. Since his will in rela-
tion to form is always directed to the whole he is not
prepared (256) in relation to matter to direct it to the
part, and yet in most cases the matters are only trifling
by which he can display his moral disposition. Thus it
not infrequently happens that because of the limitless
ideal he overlooks the application in the limited case,
and, himself imbued by a maximum, loses sight of the
minimum out of which, nevertheless, everything great
arises in actuality.

In order to do justice to the realist, therefore, one
must judge him according to the entire context of his
life; for the idealist one must limit oneself to particular
occurrences in it, but these must first be selected. Com-
mon opinion, which so gladly decides on the basis of
individual cases, will therefore maintain an indifferent
silence in regard to the realist because individual ac-
tions provide as little occasion for praise as for blame;
but in connection with the idealist, opinion will always
be partial and divided between obloquy and admira-
tion, because both his weakness and his strength lie in
his individual acts.

It is unavoidable, because of so great a divergence
of principles, that both parties will often be diametri-
cally opposed in their judgments and that, even if they
should agree as to facts and outcomes, their reasons
will be opposed. The realist will ask what a thing is
good *for*, and will appraise things according to their
use; the idealist will ask *whether* they are good, and
appraise them according to their worth. Whatever

possesses its value and purpose in itself (with the exception, however, of the whole) the realist little knows or esteems; in matters of taste his criterion will be pleasure, in matters of morality it will be happiness, even if he does not make this the condition of moral action; in his religion, too, he does not gladly forget his *interest*, but he renders it noble and sacred by the ideal of the *greatest good*. Whatever he loves he will seek to make *happy*, (257) where the idealist will seek to *ennoble* it. Whereas the realist aims, in his political tendencies at *well-being* even if it should to some extent detract from the moral self-reliance of the people, the idealist will imperil well-being to make freedom his standard. To the first, independence *of condition* is his highest object; to the second, independence *from condition*, and this characteristic difference can be traced throughout their respective modes of thought and action. Thus the realist will always manifest his affection by *giving*, the idealist by *receiving*; and each reveals by what he sacrifices in his generosity what he prizes most highly. The idealist will pay for the shortcomings of his system with his own person and with his temporal condition, but he does not esteem this sacrifice; the realist makes up for the shortcomings of his with his personal dignity, but he knows nothing of this sacrifice. His system holds good for everything about which he knows and for which he feels a need—why should he be bothered with goods of which he has no notion and in which he does not believe? It is enough for him that he is in possession, the earth is his, light dawns in his understanding, and satisfaction in his breast. The idealist by no means enjoys so happy a fate. It is not enough that he often quarrels with happiness because he fails to make the moment his friend, he quarrels with himself too; he cannot be content either with his knowledge or with his actions. What he demands of himself is boundless; but everything that he achieves is limited. This rigor, which he applies to himself, he does not renounce in his behavior towards others. He is indeed generous because in relations with others he does not remember his own individuality so much; but he is often unfair because he as easily overlooks the individuality of others. The realist, on the other hand, is less generous, but more fair-minded since he judges everything rather *in its limitation.* The vulgar, even the base in thought and action he can (258) forgive, but never the arbitrary or eccentric; but the idealist is the sworn enemy of everything petty and jejune and will reconcile himself even with the extravagant and monstrous if it only testifies to a great potentiality. The former shows himself to be a philanthropist but simply without entertaining any very high idea of humanity; the latter thinks so highly of mankind that he thereby falls into the danger of despising man.

Left to himself the realist would never extend the compass of mankind beyond the borders of the world of sense, he would never seek to acquaint the human spirit with its independent greatness and freedom; for everything absolute in humanity is for him only a beautiful chimera and belief in it is not much better than fanaticism, because he never observes men in their pure potentiality, only in a determined and hence limited actuality. But the idealist left to himself would just as little seek to cultivate the sensuous faculties or to educate man as a natural being; yet this is an equally substantial part of man's vocation and the condition of all moral ennoblement. The striving of the idealist too far surpasses the sensuous life and the present moment; only for the whole, for eternity, does he want to sow and plant, and thereby forgets that the whole is only the consummated cycle of the individual, that eternity is only a totality of moments. The world, as the realist would construct it about himself, and in fact does, is a well-planned garden in which everything has its use, and merits its place and from which everything that does not bear fruit is banished; in the hands of the idealist the world is nature less utilized, but laid out on a grander scale. It does not occur to the first that man could exist for any other purpose than to live well and contentedly, and that he puts roots down only in order to thrust the plant into the skies. The latter does not understand that he (259) should live well if only in order to think equally well and nobly, and that the plant must wither if the roots are lacking.

If in a system something is left out for which an urgent and unavoidable need exists in nature, then nature can only be satisfied by some inconsistency in the system. Here both parties are guilty of such an inconsistency and this demonstrates, even if it could still have remained in doubt hitherto, both the one-sidedness of the two systems and the richness of content of human nature. In regard to the idealist I do not have to supply any particular proof that he must necessarily depart from his system as soon as he aims at a particular effect: for all determined existence depends upon temporal conditions and follows empirical laws. With reference to the realist, however, it might seem doubtful whether he was not in fact able to do justice within his system to all the necessary demands of mankind. If one asks the realist: "Why do you do what is right, and submit to what is necessary?" he would reply in the spirit of his system: "Because this is involved in nature, because that is how it must be." But this by no means answers the question, because we are not speaking about what is involved in nature but about what men want, since they can certainly *not* want what must be. One can then ask him again: "Why do you want what must be? Why do you submit your free will to this necessity of nature since it can just as well (even without success, which we are not discussing here) be opposed to her, and in millions of your fellow men is in fact opposed? You cannot say because all other natural beings submit to her, for you for one possess a will, and even feel that your submission should be a voluntary one. You submit, then, if you do so voluntarily, not to the necessity of nature itself, but to the *idea* (260) of it; for the first merely compels you blindly as it compels the worm; but it has no power over your will, for you, even crushed by it, can still express another desire. But where do you take that idea of the necessity of nature? Surely not from experience which supplies you only with the discrete effects of nature but not with nature (as a whole), and only with discrete actualities but not with necessity. Thus you go beyond nature and determine yourself idealistically, each time you will to *act morally* or only not to *endure blindly*." It is apparent, then, that the realist acts more worthily than, following his theory, he would allow, just as the idealist thinks more sublimely than he acts. Without admitting it to himself the first displays in the whole conduct of his life the self-reliance of human nature while the latter displays its poverty in his individual actions.

To the attentive and impartial reader I will not, following the account just given (the truth of which can be admitted even by anybody who does not accept the outcome), have first to demonstrate that the ideal of human nature is divided between both, but is not fully attained by either. Experience and reason each has its own prerogatives and neither can infringe in the area of the other without inflicting serious consequences upon either the inner or external condition of man. Experience alone can teach us what is under certain conditions, what follows upon certain antecedent circumstances, and what must occur for a certain purpose. Reason alone, on the other hand, can teach us what is unconditionally valid and what must necessarily be so. If we should presume to decide anything by our pure reason about the external existence of things we should be engaged in a merely empty game, and the results would amount to nothing; for all existence is conditional and reason determines unconditionally. If, however, we should permit an accidental occurrence to decide about something that (261) is already involved in the mere concept of our own being, then we make of ourselves an empty game of chance, and our personality would amount to nothing. In the first case we relinquish the value (the temporal content) of our lives, in the second the dignity (the moral content).

In our account thus far we have indeed allowed a moral value to the realist and a measure of experience to the idealist, but only insofar as both do not proceed consistently, and nature operates in them more powerfully than their systems. Even though both do not entirely correspond to the ideal of perfect humanity, yet between them the important difference subsists that although the realist in no individual case does justice

to the rational concept of mankind, he never contra-
dicts its concept of the understanding; and although
the idealist in individual cases approaches the highest
concept of humanity, he not infrequently falls short of
even its lowest concepts. But in practical life much
more depends upon the whole being *uniformly* hu-
manly good, than upon the particular being *acciden-
tally* divine—and even if the idealist is a more appro-
priate subject to arouse in us a lofty notion of what is
possible for mankind, and to imbue us with respect for
its vocation, still only the realist can carry it out in
practice with constancy and maintain the race within
its eternal boundaries. The former is indeed a more
noble, but a disproportionately less perfect being; the
latter may appear generally less noble, but he is on the
other hand all the more perfect; for nobility is already
present in the manifestation of a great potentiality, but
the perfect lies in the conduct of the whole and in
actual need.

What is true of both characters in their most favor-
able interpretation is even more noticeable in their
respective *caricatures*. True realism is more (262)
beneficent in its effects and only less noble in its ori-
gin; false realism is contemptible in its origin and only
slightly less pernicious in its effects. For the true real-
ist submits himself to nature and to her necessity—but
to nature as a whole, to her eternal and absolute neces-
sity, not to her blind and momentary *compulsions*. He
embraces and follows her law in freedom, and will
always subordinate the particular to the universal;
thus he cannot fail to agree with the genuine idealist
in the final result, however different the path which
each takes to that end. The vulgar empiricist, however,
submits himself to nature as a force, and in indiscrimi-

nate blind surrender. His judgments, like his efforts, are
limited to the particular; he believes and grasps only
what he touches; he esteems only what advances him
sensuously. He is, therefore, no more than external
impressions chance to make him; his individuality is
suppressed and, as a human being, he possesses abso-
lutely no worth and no dignity. But as a thing he is
still something, he can still serve some purpose. For
that same nature to which he blindly abandons himself
does not let him sink altogether; her eternal boundaries
protect him, her inexhaustible assistance rescues him,
if only he surrenders his freedom short of total aban-
donment. Although in this condition he knows no laws,
yet they govern him unacknowledged, and as much as
his individual efforts might be in conflict with the
whole, yet that whole will infallibly be able to over-
come them. There are men enough, even whole peo-
ples, who live in this lamentable condition, who sur-
vive solely by the grace of the law of nature, without
individuality, and hence are good only *for something;*
but that they even live and survive demonstrates that
this condition is not entirely without meaning.

If, in contrast to this, true idealism is insecure and
often dangerous in its effects, (263) false idealism is
appalling in its effects. The true idealist abandons
nature and experience only because he does not find
in it the immutable and unconditional necessity for
which his reason prompts him to strive; the fantast
abandons nature out of mere caprice, in order to in-
dulge with all the less restraint the wantonness of his
desires and the whims of his imagination. He bases
freedom, not in independence from physical duress,
but in emancipation from moral compulsion. Thus the
fantast renounces not only human character—he re-

nounces all character, he is completely lawless, hence nothing in himself and fit for nothing. But for the very reason that his phantasmagoria is not a deviation from nature but from freedom, and this develops out of a capacity in itself estimable and infinitely perfectible, it leads likewise to an infinite fall into a bottomless abyss and can only terminate in complete destruction.

ON THE SUBLIME

ON THE SUBLIME

(264)   "No man must 'must'," the Jew Nathan says to
the Dervish,[1] and this adage is truer to a greater extent
than one would perhaps be willing to allow. The will
is the genetic characteristic of man as species, and even
reason is only its eternal rule. All nature proceeds
rationally; man's prerogative is merely that he pro-
ceeds rationally with consciousness and intent. All
other things "must"; man is the being that wills.

For just this reason nothing is so unworthy of man
than to suffer violence, for violence undoes him. Who-
ever offers us violence calls into question nothing less
than our humanity; whoever suffers this cravenly
throws his humanity away. But this claim to absolute
liberation from everything violent seems to presuppose
a being possessing force enough to repel every other
force from itself. If it is claimed by a being who does
not occupy the highest rank in the realm of force, an
unhappy contradiction arises thence between aspira-
tion and capacity.

This is the position in which man finds himself. Sur-
rounded by countless forces, all of which are superior
to his own and wield mastery over him, he lays claim
by his nature to suffer violence from none of them. He
is, indeed, enabled by his understanding artificially to
enhance his natural powers, and up to a certain point
he is actually successful in becoming the physical mas-

193

ter of everything physical. (265) There is a cure for
everything, the proverb says, except for death. But this
single exception, even if it is that in the strictest sense,
would destroy the whole concept of humanity. Man
can no longer be the being that wills if there is even a
single case in which he simply must do what he does
not will. This single terror, *which he simply must do
and does not will,* will haunt him like a specter and, as
is the case in the majority of people, will deliver him
up prey to the blind terrors of imagination; his vaunted
freedom is absolutely nothing if he is bound in even a
single point. Culture is to set man free and to help
him to be equal to his concept. It should therefore
enable him to assert his will, for man is the being that
wills.

This is possible in two ways. Either *realistically,*
when man opposes violence with violence, when he
masters nature as nature; or *idealistically,* when he
withdraws from nature and thus, as concerns himself,
overcomes the concept of violence. What aids him in
the first is called physical culture [science]. Man culti-
vates his understanding and his sensuous faculties in
order to exploit natural forces in accordance with their
own laws, either as instruments of his will, or to safe-
guard himself against those of their effects that he
cannot control. But the forces of nature can be con-
trolled or diverted only up to a certain point; beyond
this point they elude man's power and subordinate him
to themselves.

This would, then, be the end of his freedom, if he
were capable only of physical science. But he is sup-
posed to be a human being unconditionally, and should
therefore under no circumstances suffer anything

against his will. If he is no longer able to oppose physi-
cal force by his relatively weaker physical force, then
the only thing that remains to him, if he is not to suf-
fer (266) violence, is to *eliminate utterly and com-
pletely* a relationship that is so disadvantageous to
him, and *to destroy the very concept* of a force to
which he must in fact succumb. To destroy the very
concept of a force means simply to submit to it volun-
tarily. The science that enables us to do this is called
moral science.

The morally cultivated man, and only he, is wholly
free. Either he is superior to nature as a force, or he is
at one with her. Nothing that she can do to him is vio-
lence because before it reaches *him* it has already be-
come *his own action,* and dynamic nature never reaches
him, because he has by his own free act separated him-
self from everything that she can reach. This frame of
mind which morality teaches as the concept of resigna-
tion in the face of necessity, and which religion teaches
as the concept of submission to the divine judgment
requires, however, if it is to be an act of free choice
and deliberation, much more in the way of clarity of
thought and energy of volition than the individual is
accustomed to exercise in practical life. Fortunately he
possesses not only in his rational nature a moral tend-
ency that can be developed by his understanding, but
even in his sensuously reasonable (i.e., human) nature
an *aesthetic* tendency that is aroused by certain sensi-
ble objects and which by the purification of his feel-
ings can be cultivated toward this idealistic impulse of
his spirit. I now propose to treat of this tendency; one
which in its conception and being is indeed idealistic,
but which the realist also displays clearly enough in

his life, even though he does not acknowledge it in his system.*

Developed feelings for the beautiful can indeed succeed (267) up to a certain degree in making us independent of nature as a force. A mind sufficiently refined as to be moved more by the form than the matter of things and, without any reference to possession, to experience disinterested pleasure in sheer reflection upon the mode of their appearance—such a mind contains within itself an inner irrepressible fullness of life, and since it does not need to appropriate to itself those objects in which it lives, neither is it in danger of being despoiled of them. But in the final analysis even semblance [2] needs a physical substance in which it can be manifested; therefore so long as a need is present, if only for beautiful semblance, then, too, there remains a need for the *existence* of objects, and thus our satisfaction is still dependent upon nature as a power, for she rules over all existences. But it makes a great difference whether we feel a need for beautiful and good objects, or whether we merely demand that those objects that are existent be beautiful and good. The latter is consonant with the highest freedom of the spirit, but the former is not; that the existent be beautiful and good we may demand—that the beautiful and the good exist we may only wish for. That mental temperament which is indifferent whether the beautiful and the good and the perfect exist, is above all called great and sublime because it contains all the realities of the beautiful character without sharing any of its limitations.

* Indeed, nothing at all can be truly called idealistic if it is not in actuality unconsciously employed by the thoroughgoing realist, and denied by him only by a misunderstanding.

It is a touchstone of good and beautiful souls, which are nonetheless weak, always to insist impatiently upon the existence of their moral ideals, and to be painfully affected by the obstacles that balk their fulfillment. Such persons involve themselves in a sorry dependence upon coincidence, and one can always say with certainty in advance that they make too much provision for matter in moral and aesthetic things, and will not survive the highest tests of character (268) and taste. The morally defective should not imbue us with suffering and pain, which always bespeak an unsatisfied need rather than an unfulfilled demand. The latter must be accompanied by a more vital emotion and should rather strengthen the mind and confirm it in its powers than render it depressed and unhappy.[3]

Two genii are nature's gift to accompany us through life. The first, sociable and attractive, by its joyful play, shortens our tedious journey; it lightens the shackles of necessity and with gaiety and jocularity leads us up to the dangerous places where we must act as pure spirit and cast off everything physical—up to knowledge of the truth and the practice of duty. Here it leaves us, for its realm is the world of sense only and beyond this its earthly wings cannot bear us. But now the second approaches, tacit and solemn, and upon its powerful pinion we are borne across the vertiginous depths.[4]

In the first of these genii can be seen our feeling for the beautiful; and in the second our feeling for the sublime. The beautiful is indeed an expression of freedom, but not that which elevates us above the power of nature and releases us from every physical influence; rather it is the expression which we enjoy as individuals within nature. We feel ourselves free in the pres-

ence of beauty because our sensuous impulses have no
influence upon the legislation of reason, for here the
mind acts as if it were bound by no other laws than
its own.

The feeling of the sublime is a mixed feeling. It is a
composition of melancholy which at its utmost is mani-
fested in a shudder, and of joyousness which can mount
to rapture and, even if it is not actually pleasure, is far
preferred by refined souls (269) to all pleasure. This
combination of two contradictory perceptions in a
single feeling demonstrates our moral independence in
an irrefutable manner. For since it is absolutely impos-
sible for the very same object to be related to us in two
different ways, it therefore follows that *we ourselves*
are related to the object in two different ways; further-
more, two opposed natures must be united in us, each
of which is interested in diametrically opposed ways
in the perception of the object. By means of the feel-
ing for the sublime, therefore, we discover that the
state of our minds is not necessarily determined by the
state of our sensations, that the laws of nature are not
necessarily our own, and that we possess a principle
proper to ourselves that is independent of all sensuous
affects.

The sublime object is of a dual sort. We refer it
either to our *power of apprehension* and are defeated
in the attempt to form an image of its concept; or we
refer it to our *vital power* and view it as a power
against which our own dwindles to nothing.[5] But even
if, in the first case or the second, it is the occasion of a
painful awareness of our limitations, still we do not
run away from it, but rather are drawn to it by an
irresistible force. Would this be even possible if the
limits of our imagination were at the same time the

limits of our power of apprehension? Would we so gladly accede to the reminder of the overwhelming power of natural forces if we did not possess something else in reserve which need not fall prey to those forces? We delight in the sensuously infinite because we are able to think what the senses can no longer apprehend and the understanding can no longer comprehend. We are ravished by the terrifying because we are able to will that which our sensuous impulses are appalled by, and can reject what they desire. We gladly permit the (270) imagination to meet its master in the realm of appearances because ultimately it is only a sensuous faculty that triumphs over other sensuous faculties; but nature in her entire boundlessness cannot impinge upon the absolute greatness within ourselves. We gladly subordinate our well-being and our existence to physical necessity, for we are reminded thereby that it cannot command our principles. Man is in its hands, but man's will is in his own hands.

Thus Nature has even employed a sensuous means of teaching us that we are more than merely sensuous; she even succeeds in so applying our perceptions as to afford us a clue to the discovery that we are anything but slavishly subordinate to the force of perceptions. And this effect is quite other than that yielded by beauty—that is, by the beauty of actuality, for the sublime itself must disappear before ideal beauty. In the beautiful, reason and sensuousness are in unison, and only for the sake of this harmony does it possess any charm for us. Through beauty alone, then, we should never discover that we are destined and able to manifest ourselves as pure intelligences. But in the sublime, however, reason and sensuousness do *not* accord, and precisely in this contradiction between the two lies the magic with which it captures our minds. The physical and the moral individual are here most sharply differentiated from one another; for it is precisely in the presence of objects that make the former aware only of his limitations that the latter is aware of his *power* and is infinitely exalted by the very same object that crushes the physical man to the ground.

A man should, I suppose, possess all the virtues that, in unison, make for a *beautiful character*. He should find delight in the practice of righteousness, beneficence, moderation, perseverance, and loyalty; all duties, obedience to which are (271) indicated by circumstances, should be an easy play for him, and his happiness should render no action whatever difficult for him that his philanthropic heart prompts him to undertake. Who could fail to be enchanted by this fair accord of natural impulses with the prescriptions of reason; and who could restrain himself from loving such a man? Even if this man had set his mind only on pleasant sensations he still could not, without being a fool, act otherwise, and would be forced to slight his own advantage if he wanted to be sinful. It may be that the source of his actions is pure—but this he must settle within his own heart—*we* see nothing of this. We see him doing no more than the merely shrewd man must do who has made pleasure his god. The world of sense thus explains the whole phenomenon of his virtue and we do not find it necessary to go beyond that world to find a reason for his virtue.

But let us suppose this same man suddenly to suffer a great misfortune. Let him be robbed of his possessions, let his good reputation be destroyed. Sickness might reduce him to a bed of pain, death may tear from him all he loves, he may be abandoned in his distress by all he trusts. Under these circumstances let us seek him out and demand of the unhappy wretch that he practise the same virtues to which the happy man was formerly so inclined. If, under these circumstances, one should find him altogether the same, if poverty has not diminished his beneficence, ingratitude his readiness to be of service, pain his equanimity, his own misfortune his satisfaction in the happiness of others— if we notice the change in his fortune by his outward appearance but not in his behavior, in the substance but not in the form of his (272) actions—then, indeed, no explanation can suffice that depends on a *natural concept* (in accordance with which it follows by simple necessity that the present as effect must be based on something in the past as cause), for nothing can be more contradictory than that the effect should remain the same when the cause has changed to its opposite. We must then reject any natural explanation, we must abandon completely the derivation of behavior from circumstances and locate the reason for the behavior not in the physical world-order, but in quite another to which the ideas of reason can indeed soar, but which understanding cannot apprehend by its empirical concepts. This discovery of the absolute moral capacity which is not bound to any natural condition endows the melancholy feeling by which we are seized at the spectacle of such a man with the unique and ineffable charm which no pleasure of sense, however refined it might be, can offer in competition with the sublime.

Thus the sublime affords us an egress from the sensuous world in which the beautiful would gladly hold us forever captive. Not gradually (for there is no transition from dependence to freedom), but suddenly [6] and with a shock it tears the independent spirit out of

the net in which a refined sensuousness has entoiled it,
and which binds all the more tightly the more gos-
samer its weave. If by the imperceptible influence of a
vitiated taste it has gained however strong a hold—
even if in the seductive guise of the spiritually beauti-
ful it has succeeded in penetrating the innermost seat
of moral legislation, there to poison the holiness of its
maxims at their source, often a single sublime emotion
suffices to rip this web of deceit asunder, to restore in
an instant all the vivacity of the bound spirit, to accord
it a revelation of its true vocation, and, for the mo-
ment at least, to impose upon it a sense of its dignity.
(273) The beauty displayed by the figure of the god-
dess Calypso enchanted the brave son of Ulysses, and
by the power of her charms she long held him captive
on her island. For a long time he believed he was wor-
shiping an immortal divinity, yet he lay only in the
arms of lust—but suddenly a sublime impression over-
came him in the guise of Mentor: he recollected his
higher mission, cast himself into the waves, and was
free.[7]

The sublime, like the beautiful, is prodigally diffused
throughout the whole of nature and the capacity to
apprehend both is implanted in all men; but the poten-
tiality to do so is unequally developed and must be
aided by art. The very purpose of nature entails that
we hasten toward beauty when we still only flee from
the sublime; for beauty is our caretaker in the years of
childhood and must lead us out of the crude state of
nature into refinement. But even if beauty is our first
love and our capacity of apprehending it develops
first, yet nature has provided that it only slowly ma-
ture and await for its complete development the mat-
uration of the understanding and the heart. For if

taste should attain complete maturity before truth and morality are implanted in our hearts in a manner better than beauty can supply, then the world of sense would forever remain the limit of our aspirations. Neither in our concepts nor in our attitudes should we be able to go beyond that world, and what the faculty of imagination could not envisage would likewise possess no reality for us. But fortunately it is among the provisions of nature that although taste is the first to bloom it must wait for its ripening last among all the faculties of mind. In this interval sufficient time is gained for a treasure of concepts to be implanted in the head and a wealth of principles in the breast and thereafter to develop especially the capacity (274) to apprehend the great and sublime by means of reason.

So long as man was merely a slave of physical necessity, had not yet found an egress from the narrow sphere of his wants, and still did not suspect the lofty *daemonic* freedom in his breast, he was reminded by *inscrutable* nature only of the inadequacy of his conceptual faculties and by *destructive* nature only of his physical incapacity. The first he was obliged humbly to acknowledge and from the second he turned in revulsion. But no sooner has free contemplation set him at a distance from the blind assault of natural forces— no sooner does he discover in the flood of appearances something abiding in his own being—then the savage bulk of nature about him begins to speak quite another language to his heart; and the relative grandeur outside him is the mirror in which he perceives the absolute grandeur within himself. Fearlessly and with a terrible delight he now approaches these ghastly visions of his imagination and deliberately deploys the whole force of this faculty in order to represent the sensuously infinite, so that even if it should fail in this attempt he will experience all the more vividly the superiority of his ideas over the highest of which sensuousness is capable. The sight of unlimited distances, and heights lost to view, the vast ocean at his feet and the vaster ocean above him, pluck his spirit out of the narrow sphere of the actual and out of the oppressive bondage of physical life. A mightier measure of esteem is exemplified for him by the simple majesty of nature, and surrounded by her massive forms he can no longer tolerate pettiness in his mode of thought. Who knows how many illumined thoughts or heroic decisions that could never have been born in a cell-like study or a society salon have been produced out of this bold struggle of the mind with the great spirit of nature while wandering abroad—who knows whether it is in part due to the rare commerce with (275) this great genius that the character of the city dweller so gladly turns, lame and sere, to the jejune, while the mind of the nomad remains as open and free as the firmament beneath which he camps.

8 But it is not merely what is unattainable for imagination, the sublime of quantity, but what is incomprehensible for the understanding, *confusion,* that can likewise serve as a representation of the supersensuous and supply the mind with an upward impetus, provided it advances to greatness and announces itself as a work of nature (for otherwise it is contemptible). Who does not prefer to tarry among the spiritual disorder of a natural landscape rather than in the spiritless regularity of a French garden? Who would not marvel at the wonderful battle between fecundity and destruction in Sicily's plains, or feast his eyes on Scotland's wild cataracts and mist-shrouded mountains, Os-

sian's vast nature, rather than admire in straight-diked Holland the prim victory of patience over the most defiant of the elements? Nobody will deny that better care is taken of physical man in the meadows of Batavia than beneath the treacherous crater of Vesuvius, and that an understanding that wishes to comprehend and classify will much more readily be satisfied in a planned commercial garden than in a savage natural landscape. But man has a need beyond living and securing his welfare, and quite another destiny than to comprehend the phenomena that surround him.

What makes the bizarre savagery in physical creation so attractive to the sensitive traveler likewise represents the source of a quite unique pleasure for a mind capable of delight even in the uncertain anarchy of the moral world. It is true that anyone who illuminates the vast economy of nature with the pale light of understanding, and whose only concern is to resolve its bold disorder into harmony, will not be satisfied in a world in which crass (276) coincidence rather than a wise plan seems to rule, and in by far the majority of cases merit and reward stand in a contradictory relation. He demands that everything in the world be regulated as in a solid business and if he fails to find this obedience to rule (as can scarcely be otherwise) then nothing remains to him but to expect from a future existence and from another nature that satisfaction that he misses in present and past nature. If, however, he willingly abandons the attempt to assimilate this lawless chaos of appearances to a cognitive unity, he will abundantly regain in another direction what he has lost in this. It is precisely the entire absence of a purposive bond among this press of appearances by which they are rendered unencompassable and useless for the understanding (which is obliged to adhere to this kind of bond) that makes them an all the more striking image for pure reason, which finds in just this wild incoherence of nature the depiction of her own independence of natural conditions. For if the connection among a series of objects is abstracted, one is left with the concept of independence which coincides surprisingly with the pure rational concept of freedom. Thus reason combines in a single unity of thought within this idea of freedom, which she supplies from her own resources, what understanding can never combine in a unity of experience; by this idea she subordinates the infinite play of appearances to herself, and simultaneously asserts her power over the understanding as a sensuously limited faculty. If one now recalls how valuable it must be for a rational being to be aware of his independence of natural laws, one can grasp how it happens that individuals of a sublime temperamental disposition think themselves recompensed for every cognitive misjudgment by this idea of freedom which is offered them. To noble minds freedom, for all its moral contradictions and physical evils, is (277) an infinitely more interesting spectacle than prosperity and order without freedom, when the sheep patiently follow the shepherd and the autonomous will reduces itself to an obedient cog in a machine. The latter makes of man a mere product of nature's ingenuity and her fortunate subject; but freedom makes him a citizen and co-regent of a higher system in which it is incomparably more honorable to occupy the lowest rank than to lead the procession of the physical order.

Viewed from this aspect and *only* from this, world history appears to me a sublime object. The world, as an historical subject matter, is basically nothing but the conflict of natural forces among themselves and with man's freedom; history reports to us the outcome of this battle. As history has thus far developed, it has much greater deeds to recount about nature (in which all human emotions must be included) than about independent reason which has asserted its power only in a few exceptions to the natural law, such as Cato, Aristides, Phocian, and similar men. Should one approach history with great expectations of illumination and knowledge—how very disappointed one is! All the well-intentioned attempts of philosophy to reconcile what the moral world *demands* with what it actually *performs* are contradicted by the testimony of experience, and, as amiably as nature in her *organic realm* is guided, or appears to be guided, by the regulative principles of judgment, in the realm of freedom she as impetuously tears off the reins by which the speculative spirit would gladly lead her.

How different it is if one abandons the possibility of *explaining* Nature and takes this incomprehensibility itself as a principle of judgment. The very circumstance that nature, viewed as a whole, mocks all the rules that (278) we prescribe for her by our understanding—that in her obdurately free advance she treads into the dust the creations of wisdom and of chance with equal indifference; that she drags down with her in a *single* collapse both the important and the trivial; that here she preserves a community of ants, while there she enfolds in her arms and crushes her most splendid creature, man; that she often wastes in a wanton hour the most tediously won achievements, while often working for centuries on some inane labor—in a word, this disregard by nature as a whole of the laws of science (which she obeys in individual cases) renders obvious the absolute impossibility of explaining *nature herself* by means of *natural laws,* and of imputing *to* her domain what holds *in* her domain, and thus the mind is irresistibly driven out of the world of phenomena into the world of ideas, out of the conditioned into the unconditioned.

We are led much further by nature viewed as terrible and destructive than as sensuously infinite, provided we remain merely free observers of her. The sensuous man certainly, and the sensuousness in the rational man fear nothing so much as to be destroyed by that power that rules over prosperity and existence.

The highest ideal to which we aspire is to remain on good terms with the physical world as the executrix of our happiness, without thereby being obliged to fall out with the moral world that determines our dignity. Now it is well known how rarely one can succeed in serving two masters, and even if (an almost impossible case) duty should never conflict with physical need, still natural necessity has entered into no compact with man, and neither his strength nor his skill can protect him against the treachery of fate. Let him be happy if he has learned to bear what he cannot (279) alter, and to surrender with dignity what he cannot save! Cases can occur in which fate surmounts all the ramparts upon which man founds his security and nothing else remains but for him to flee into the sacred freedom of the spirit [9]—cases in which there is no other recourse in order to placate the lust for life than to will that fate—and no other means of withstanding the power of nature than to anticipate her, and by a free renunciation of all sensuous interest to kill himself morally before some physical force does it.

He is strengthened in this by sublime emotions and by frequent acquaintance with destructive nature, both where she shows him her ruinous strength only from afar and when she actually employs it against his fellow man. The pathetic is an artificial misfortune, and like real misfortune it sets us in *direct concourse* with the spiritual law that rules within our breast. But true misfortune does not always choose its man nor its time well; it frequently surprises us *unarmed*. The artificial misfortune of the pathetic on the other hand finds us fully armed and, since it is only imagined, the autonomous principle in our minds gains space in which to assert its absolute independence.[10] The more frequently the mind repeats this act of independence the more skilled it becomes, the greater the advance won over the sensuous impulse, so that finally, should an imaginary and artificial misfortune turn into a real one, the mind is able to treat it as an artificial one, and—most exalted inspiration of human nature!—to transform actual suffering into sublime emotion. Thus one can call the pathetic an inoculation against ineluctable destiny by which it is deprived of its malevolence, and its attack diverted to the stronger side of man.

Then away with falsely construed forebearance and vapidly effeminate taste which cast a veil over the (280) solemn face of necessity and, in order to curry favor with the senses, *counterfeit* a harmony between good fortune and good behavior of which not a trace is to be found in the actual world. Let us stand face to face with the evil fatality. Not in ignorance of the dangers which lurk about us—for finally there must be an end to ignorance—only in *acquaintance* with them lies our salvation. We are aided in this acquaintance

by the terrifying and magnificent spectacle of change
which destroys everything and creates it anew, and
destroys again—of ruin sometimes accomplished by
slow undermining, sometimes by swift incursion. We
are aided by the pathetic spectacle of mankind wres-
tling with fate, the irresistible elusiveness of happi-
ness, confidence betrayed, unrighteousness triumphant
and innocence laid low; of these history supplies am-
ple instances, and tragic art imitates them before our
eyes. For where is the man whose moral disposition is
not wholly degenerate who can read about the deter-
mined yet vain struggle of Mithridates, of the collapse
of Syracuse and Carthage, or in the presence of like
events can refrain from paying homage with a shudder
to the grim law of necessity, or from instantly curb-
ing his desires and, shaken by the perpetual infidelity
of all sensuous objects, can avoid fastening upon the
eternal in his breast? The capability of perceiving the
sublime is thus one of the most splendid propensities
of human nature, which because of its origin in the
independent faculties of thought and volition is worthy
both of our respect and of the most perfect develop-
ment because of its influence on man as moral. The
beautiful is valuable only with reference to the *human
being*, but the sublime with reference to the *pure
daemon* in him; and since it is certainly our vocation,
despite all sensuous limitations, to be guided by the
statutes of pure spirit, the sublime must complement
the beautiful in order to make *aesthetic* (281) *educa-
tion* into a complete whole and to enlarge the percep-
tive capacity of the human heart to the full extent
of our vocation; beyond the world of sense in any
case.

Without the beautiful there would be a ceaseless

quarrel between our natural and rational vocations. In the attempt to be equal to our *spiritual mission* we should be false to our *humanity,* and, prepared at every moment for departure out of the world of sense, we should always remain strangers in the sphere of action to which we are after all committed. Without the sublime, beauty would make us forget our dignity. The enervation of uninterrupted enjoyment would cost us all vitality of *character* and, irremediably shackled to this *contingent form of existence,* we should lose sight of our immutable vocation and our true patrimony. Only if the sublime is wedded to the beautiful and our sensitivity for both has been cultivated in equal measure are we perfect citizens of nature without thereby becoming her slaves and without squandering our citizenship in the intelligible world.

Now it is true that nature herself supplies objects in abundance on which the perceptive faculty for the beautiful and sublime can be exercised; but man is here, as in other cases, better served at one remove than directly, and prefers to receive a subject matter prepared and selected by art rather than to drink scantily and with difficulty from the impure well of nature. The mimetic creative impulse, which can experience no *impression* without at once striving for a living *expression,*[11] and which sees in every beautiful or vast form of nature a challenge to contend with it, possesses the great advantage over nature of being able to treat as a major purpose and a totality in itself what nature—if she does not heedlessly reject it— (282) in passing sweeps along with her in pursuit of some more immediate purpose of her own. Nature in her beautiful organic forms either *suffers violence* because of the imperfect individuality of matter or by the effects of heterogeneous forces, or she *exercises violence* in her great and pathetic scenes and affects men as a force. Since nature can be aesthetic only as an object of free contemplation her imitator, creative art, is completely free, because it can separate from its subject matter all contingent limitations, and also leaves the mind of the observer free because it imitates only the *semblance*, and not the *actuality*. But because the whole magic of the sublime and the beautiful subsists only in semblance, art thus possesses all the advantages of nature without sharing her shackles.

NOTES

INTRODUCTION

1 *Letters on the Aesthetic Education of Man,* 2nd Letter;
XII 7, 10. All references to Schiller's works are to his
Sämtliche Werke, Säkular-Ausgabe (16 vols., Stuttgart and
Berlin, Cotta: 1904-05). All translations are my own, un-
less otherwise stated.

2 Nor is there any reference in the *Conversations with Eck-
ermann;* but in Goethe's *Annals, Jubiläumsausgabe,* XXX,
390, Goethe speaks of "certain harsh passages in *Grace
and Dignity."*

3 Elizabeth Wilkinson has urged the use of the translation
"sentimentive" to avoid the pejorative connotations of "sen-
timental" in English and to preserve an analogous distinc-
tion in German between *sentimentalisch* and *sentimental.*
Despite the respect for Professor Wilkinson's opinion that
every student of Schiller must feel, I find the coinage un-
easy and the desire to eliminate all the distaste associated
with "sentimental" misplaced in view of Schiller's ironical
preference for the naive poets, even though he is a senti-
mental poet himself. Perhaps the reminder that Schiller's
usage is like Sterne's in the *Sentimental Journey* and Flau-
bert's in his *Éducation Sentimentale* will keep matters in
perspective.

4 These subdivisions do not appear in the original text, but
are supplied here to make it easier to follow the argument.

5 "Genius is the talent (natural gift) which gives the rule to
art. Since this talent, as an innate productive capacity of
the artist, itself belongs to nature, it might thus be formu-
lated: Genius is the innate disposition of mind (*ingenium*)
by which nature supplies the rule to art." (Kant, *Critique
of Judgment,* § 46, trl. Bernard).
"As soon as [the poet] begins to work, the subject, and

nothing but the subject, must be the predominant idea in
his soul. In this moment he should avoid having his rules
all too clearly in view. They should not hold the imagina-
tive power in rein, but should point the way only at a dis-
tance, and call after it when it is in danger of going
astray. Thus they can set the lesser genius at the side of
the greater, and teach the poet what his spirit was perhaps
too narrow to perceive. (Moses Mendelssohn, *Letters Con-
cerning the Perceptions*, 4th Letter).

6   Later in the essay (205, 16) he attributes to Rousseau the
error of supposing that men need to go backwards in time
to return to a state which could only regain nature at the
price of reason. Compare a "prayer" of Rousseau's from
his early *Discours sur les Sciences et les Arts*: "Almighty
God, Who holds all spirits in Thy hands, deliver us from
the insights and the dark arts of our fathers, and restore to
us ignorance, innocence, and poverty, the only goods that
can make for our happiness and that are precious in your
sight."

7   This is not the only attack on the critics—there is an allu-
sion (184, 24) to the disputes between Lessing and Gott-
sched—the latter was "naive enough" to praise the third-
hand imitations of "classic" style, and to recommend them
to German poets as a model. Cf. also Schiller's review of
Goethe's *Iphigenia auf Tauris* (XVI 196, 5)

8   Cf. *On the Sublime* (*Über das Erhabene*) XII 277, 11,
and the discussion below for a more explicit statement on
this point.

9   Cf. XII 195, 12.

10 See also 196, 21.

11 This is a clear anticipation of the argument of *On the
Sublime:* the truth about the world, its processes and pur-
poses, is strictly unknowable; we are therefore free to de-
cide what our attitude towards it shall be, whether tragic
or otherwise; aesthetic education enables us to make the
best choice. Cf. discussion below.

12 Cf. Schiller's letter to Goethe of March 18, 1796: "At first
my feelings have no specific and clear object; this devel-
ops later. First comes a certain musical mood, and only
after this my poetic idea follows." More "musical" poets,
like Hölderlin or Keats sustain a tone of lyric abandon
that is denied to Schiller.

13 These are undoubtedly the passages that made Goethe un-
comfortable (cf. his letter to Schiller of December 9, 1795,
cited above); certainly *Götz* and the *Roman Elegies* con-
tain a number of "liberties" which Goethe saw little point
in explaining.

14 F.H. Bradley, *Appearance and Reality* (London, 1893),
xiv.

15 See Note on the controversial dating of this piece.

16 Cf. *Aesthetic Letters* 25, XII 101, 22; *Naive and Senti-
mental Poetry,* XII 174, 18, and 252, 20.

17 "Chance" is not defined except in terms of unpredictabil-
ity; but the context makes it clear that it is *not* to be de-
fined in terms of merely unknown, but determinate fac-
tors.

18 This essay contains what seems to be Schiller's last word
on the subject of history (cf. 277, 11). In his two great
histories—*The Fall of the Netherlands* and *The Thirty
Years' War*—his notions of historiography, which were
very advanced for their time, certainly include a higher
destiny which appears as a pattern of universal history.
Now he finds this idea less plausible, presumably because
theories of history, like all the others we are considering,
are not given along with the facts they purport to explain,
but are unverifiable hypotheses.

19 "Thus poetry was accorded the autonomous potentiality of
apprehending life and the world: it was elevated to an in-
strument of understanding of the world and set at the side
of religion and science. The first to undertake the articula-
tion in a formula of the nature of this aesthetic originality
was Schiller." Wilhelm Dilthey, *Gesammelte Schriften*
(Stuttgart, 1958), VI, 116.

20 Shelley expresses much the same thought in his *Defence of
Poetry:* "Poetry is that which comprehends all science, and
that to which all science must be referred."

NAIVE AND SENTIMENTAL POETRY

1 This distinction will become important later: it points to a
subjective or typological difference in what nature is taken
to be rather than some uniform notion of what nature *is*.

2   This should not be taken as an appeal, like Rousseau's, to mindless happiness. Later in the essay Schiller makes clear that there is no going back to a Golden Age which never existed, but forward to the fulfilment of an ideal.

3   Sterne's work (1768) was available in German translation and had inspired a good deal of self-conscious imitation; e.g., Moritz August von Thümmel, *Reise in die mittäglichen Provinzen von Frankreich im Jahr 1785-6.*

4   "Determination" (*Bestimmung*) and "determinacy" (*Bestimmbarkeit*) refer respectively to the extent to which maturity has resulted in an actualization of possibilities, and to the range of those possibilities as potentialities that may still be realized. Cf. *Letters on the Aesthetic Education of Man*, Letters 19 and 21.

5   The terms added by Schiller in parentheses should be understood in their Kantian sense: "theoretical" refers to cognition, "practical" to morality.

6   *Affekt*: the term is still used in modern psychology, where it retains the meaning intended here: spontaneous feeling or reaction.

7   In the second of these three examples illustrating naivety of temperament, Schiller shows the peculiar vulnerability of the good man in a wicked world. This is a recurrent theme with him, as seen in the contrast between Karl and Franz Moor, Don Carlos and Philip, Wallenstein and Octavio.

8   The life of Hadrian VI (Pope, 1522-23) was known to Schiller from J.M. Schröckh's *Allgemeine Biographie,* 1767-78. The whole passage shows Schiller's expository style as an historian at its best.

9   This passage bears on the quarrel with Fichte, whom Schiller accused in a letter of June 1795 of tediousness and excessive abstraction in graceless philosophical language. Echoes of this dispute, which helped to disenchant Schiller with philosophy, are also found in another essay of this period, *Ueber die notwendigen Grenzen beim Gebrauch schöner Formen,* XII, 121 ff.

10 This paradox fascinated Schiller; he returns to it in No. 41 of the *Votivtafeln*:
    Warum kann der lebendige Geist dem Geist nicht erscheinen?

Spricht die Seele, so spricht, ach! schon *die Seele* nicht mehr.

Why cannot living spirit appear to mind?

If the soul *speaks,* then, alas! it is not *the soul* that speaks. (I, 149)

11 I.e., freedom of the will.

12 Compare the language of these oblique allusions to the as yet unnamed Goethe with the letter to Körner of February 2, 1789 quoted in the Introduction.

13 The reference is probably to Gottsched, Lessing's old enemy, who had recommended a singularly pedantic French style as a model for German dramatists to imitate. In a letter to Goethe, Schiller admits organizing "a little rabbit hunt against the critics" in this essay, in part to pay them back for their criticisms of him.

14 This characterization of Ariosto as a sentimental poet is no doubt more accurate than his inclusion among naive geniuses a few pages ago; but even Homer nods!

15 Cf. Schiller's review of Goethe's *Iphigenia* (XVI 196, 5).

16 Cf. *Aesthetic Education,* 24th Letter (XII 92, 17), where this distinction is elaborated.

17 In a letter of December 18, 1795, Wilhelm von Humboldt asked Schiller for this disquisition and was referred to the *Aesthetic Letters.* From the context it would seem that the 17th Letter is meant, especially the passage (XII 64, 5) in which he talks of the ideal of humanity and the ideal of beauty being simultaneously given.

18 This argument is expanded in the last section of the essay in the treatment of didacticism and hedonism as the "purpose" of art (cf. XII 243, 38). There, however, these two extremes are more closely associated with the naive and sentimental, and not, as here, with the two kinds of satire.

19 Schiller points to a question as applicable to the theater of our day as it was of his: whether the dramatist's work reflects a legitimate, if passionately pessimistic, view of human nature; or merely the disarray of his own personality?

20 Albrecht von Haller (1708-77), professor of physiology in Göttingen; his ideas are apparent in Schiller's thesis for the medical doctorate. Haller was also a well known poet in his day; elsewhere Schiller quotes his satiric poem *On the Origin of Evil.*

21   This expression (*Tugend des Temperaments*) does not oc-
     cur in Schiller's writings outside this paragraph. What he
     means by it, I think, is. the sort of virtue displayed in the
     absence of temptation, but on which the individual preens
     himself if anyone should notice.

22   Lucian (c. 125-180), the brilliant Greek satirist, quoted by
     Schiller in his friend Wieland's translation.

23   "Yorick" is Lawrence Sterne.

24   Ewald von Kleist (1715-59) was a lyricist and also the
     author of patriotic poetry; he was killed in battle.

25   James Thomson, whose *Seasons* were enormously popular
     in Germany in a translation by Barthold Heinrich Brockes.

25ª Edward Young (1683-1765), English poet, author of a
     series of elegies, *Night Thoughts* (1742-5) which contrib-
     uted considerable impetus to the Romantic movement in
     Germany and France.

26   Klopstock, who by now is almost unreadable, is not really
     worthy of most of this criticism. It should instead be taken
     as an elaboration of Schiller's difficulties with the "musi-
     cal" mood. As it applies to Klopstock, what is meant is ex-
     treme woolliness of thought and what Melville called "de-
     testable allegory."

26ª Harp, lyre, lute: symbols of epic, lyric, and elegiac poetry
     respectively.

27   Johann Peter Uz (1720-96) and Georg Jacobi (1740-
     1814) were "Anacreontics"; Michael Denis (1729-1800)
     and Heinrich Wilhelm Gerstenberg (1737-1823) were
     members of the "bardic" movement, the latter is famous
     for his early Storm and Stress tragedy *Ugolino;* Salomon
     Gessner (1730-87); Ludwig Hölty (1748-76); Leopold
     Friedrich Göckingk (1748-1828).

28   *Wilhelm Meister.*

29   This refers to the Fragment of 1790, which was all that
     was published of *Faust* so far.

30   I.e., 1777, the date of Johann Martin Miller's *Siegwart,
     Eine Klostergeschichte,* referred to in the next paragraph.

31   Cf. note 3.

32   "German Ovid": Johann Kaspar Friedrich Manso, cf.
     Xenien 28-33; Crébillon: probably the son (1707-77) is

intended—he emerged from jail for writing immoral novels to become Royal Censor; Jean-François Marmontel (1728-99), secretary of the Académie; Choderlos de Laclos (1741-1803), author of *Les Liaisons Dangereuses*. These represent the debit side of this attempt to balance the autonomy of art against obscenity. On the credit side is the "German Propertius," Goethe, whose *Roman Elegies* offended the straitlaced and, in the note below, Wieland.

33   This "more detailed exposition" was never written. Cf. the letter to Wilhelm von Humboldt of November 29, 1795.

34   Rousseau is, of course, intended. Cf. note 6 of the Introduction.

35   Two idylls by Gessner; possibly *Amyntas* refers to a pastoral poem by Tasso that had been translated into German a year before this essay.

36   Johann Jakob Bodmer (1698-1783) produced Old Testament epics in weak imitation of Klopstock's *Messiah*.

37   Ludvig Holberg (1684-1754), founder of the Danish National Theater; Johann Elias Schlegel (1718-49), uncle of the brothers Wilhelm and Friedrich; Johann Gellert (1715-69), novelist and author of popular comedies; Gottlieb Wilhelm Rabener (1747-71), a satirist.

38   The three rivers are an oblique reference to the places of publication of the Leipzig, Göttingen, and the Vossische Almanacks, rivals of Schiller's journal. In the note, the anonymous reviewer of Bürger's poems was Schiller himself (cf. XVI 229 ff.)

39   Christian Salzmann produced this in 1784-88.

40   An allusion to Friedrich Nicolai's *Story of a Fat Man* (1784). Nicolai was a popular hack, and a frequent victim of Schiller and Goethe in the *Xenien*.

41   St. Preux: the hero of Rousseau's *La nouvelle Héloise;* the last three are mentioned in Wieland's *Musarion*.

42   The Muses of Comedy and Tragedy respectively.

ON THE SUBLIME

1 In Lessing's *Nathan the Wise*, I, 3.

2 *Schein;* cf. *Aesthetic Education*, Letter 26, I 104, 29, and Introduction.

3 This passage probably refers to Rousseau; cf. *Naive and Sentimental Poetry*, XII 205, 11 ff.

4 This is a close paraphrase of the poem *Die Führer des Lebens* (*The Guides of Life*), I 260.

5 "Power of apprehension" (*Fassungskraft*) and "vital power" (*Lebenskraft*) refer respectively to our cognitive powers and to the faculty of judgment in the Kantian sense.

6 In *Fear and Trembling* Kierkegaard makes a similar point of the sudden and unexpected transition from the aesthetic to the ethical point of view in a context not far removed from Schiller's remarks on the beautiful and the sublime.

7 Not Homer! This tale follows Fénélon's *Les Aventures de Télémaque, fils d'Ulysse* (1699); cf. the conclusion of Book VII.

8 From here to the end of the essay I take to be a later addition, probably just before publication in 1801. See the Note on the text.

9 Cf. *Das Ideal und das Leben* (*The Ideal and Life*), vv. 101 ff., I, 194.

10 Cf. *On the Pathetic*, especially XI 262, 35, where the discussion centers about the Kantian account of the sublime.

11 Cf. *Die Künstler (The Artists)*, vv. 133 ff., I, 180.